PAPER COLLECTIBLES
THE ESSENTIAL BUYER'S GUIDE

PAPER COLLECTIBLES
THE ESSENTIAL BUYER'S GUIDE

Robert Reed

Wallace-Homestead Book Company
Radnor, Pennsylvania

Designed by Stan Green
Manufactured in the United States of America

Library of Congress Cataloging in Publication Data

Reed, Robert, 1940–
    Paper collectibles : the essential buyer's guide / Robert Reed.
        p.   cm.
    Includes index.
    ISBN 0-87069-718-8
    1. Printed ephemera—United States—Catalogs.   2. Printed
ephemera—Collectors and collecting—United States—Catalogs.
I. Title.
NC1284.U6R44   1995   94-27448
769.5—dc20   CIP

1 2 3 4 5 6 7 8 9 0   4 3 2 1 0 9 8 7 6 5

96371 ✓

CONTENTS

PART II—BUYER'S GUIDE
. . . .

ACKNOWLEDGMENTS

Preparing this manuscript would have been an exceedingly lonely task without my loving wife and astute business partner, Claudette Swengel Reed. Her months of assistance on this work was profoundly helpful and deeply appreciated.

A special thanks to Hake's Americana & Collectibles—an auction house which has specialized in popular-culture collectibles for over 25 years—for their support in providing illustrations used in this book. To receive a catalog for one of their 3,000-item mail and phone bid auctions, send $7.50 to Hake's Americana, PO Box 1444M, York, PA 17405.

We also wish to express appreciation to Swann Galleries, Inc. and their director of communications, Caroline Birenbaum, for steadfastly providing years of vital information and photographs. We also acknowledge our own firm, Antique and Collectible News Service, for providing a number of photographs and much of the original material, which was very professionally photographed and processed by 7 Seas in Greenfield, Indiana.

Special thanks also to 7 Seas Printing, Greenfield, Indiana, Ron Purcell and crew of Heartland Antiques, Knightstown, Indiana, and Barry and Barbara Carter of the Knightstown (Indiana) Antique Mall for wonderful advice and access to materials.

We gratefully acknowledge information and values from *Paper Collector's Monthly, Paper Pile Quarterly,* Cohasco, Inc., History Makers, Karl and Gene's Historical Originals, Ken Prag, East Coast Books, Lenore's TV Guides, Miscellaneous Man, The Political Gallery, David Newell Shaker Literature, *News, Views & Price Trends, Non-Sports Update,* Tuff Stuff's Collect, *Card Collector's Price Guide,* Strong Museum, and Webb's Antique Malls.

INTRODUCTION

As this book was being completed, a representative of the Fox television network called me to see what this edition was all about. The network was planning some special segments dealing with collecting and was trying to develop well in advance some type of programming that would, hopefully, interest viewers.

What I found out was that even after months and months of developing material for this book, it was very difficult to explain paper collectibles in the course of a telephone conversation. Actually, it took many conversations with some very nice television people who live in quite a different world from mine, but that is another story.

For me the challenge was essentially presenting the many faces of paper collectibles in this book as they appeared in the past and the present—and, hopefully, in the future. It was my opportunity to select the best of those from a collector's standpoint, now and tomorrow. The purpose was to include basic areas of modern life, including sports, official business, advertising, entertainment, political, popular culture, and holidays, and the collectible paper related to them. Also included were specific vehicles of paper, such as photographs, postcards, and trading cards, which have been so enduring and will continue to be popular into the next century.

It was my intention to stand at the shoulder of the potential buyer who was interested in exploring and enjoying the collectible potential of paper goods from advertising to trading cards. As a result this book is presented from the collector's viewpoint, including what I feel is a realistic look at retail prices in the vast and varying marketplace. The prices come, literally, from what was for sale, all the way from the neighborhood antiques mall to the nation's leading auction galleries. We have included auction prices, antiques mall prices, advertised prices of successful dealers, scores of mail-order catalogs, and three legal notepads full gathered from well-documented private sources.

None of the prices in this book were taken from price guides. Duplication may have occurred only if we looked, by chance, in the same place as other authors. Personally, I think price guides are great, but I wanted to give readers an entirely different resource with only a price sampling.

An eminent psychiatrist once wrote that the reason otherwise normal people talk to themselves is a primal need to hear the human voice. I believe the reason otherwise normal people are moved to acquire paper collectibles is their need to preserve something of past days, no matter how vital or how mundane. A century ago Victorians pasted their paper treasures in scrapbooks; today we place them behind special glass, decorate with them, or secure them in special cabinets. A century from now the methods and displays may be still different, but that bright human motivation to collect and appreciate wonderful things of paper will still be thriving.

Robert Reed
PO Box 204
Knightstown, IN 46148

Part I

Collector's Guide

· · · · · · · · · · · · · · · · · · · ·

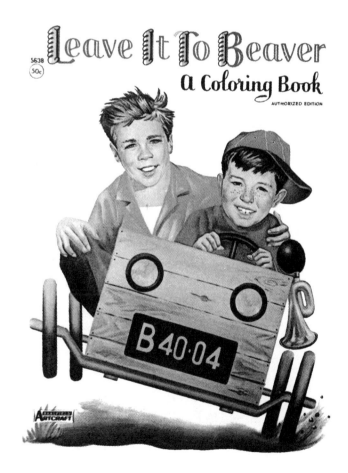

Leave It To Beaver
A Coloring Book
AUTHORIZED EDITION

5638
50¢

B 40·04

CHAPTER ONE

The Past of Paper Collectibles

*"We live in reference to past experience, and
not future events, however inevitable."*
—H.G. Wells

• •

THE HISTORY OF PAPER AND EARLY PUBLICATIONS

Paper in our civilization is old; the collecting of it is not.

Paper has flourished for thousands of years and stands in life terms as the scholarly senior citizen eligible for pension, privileges, and honors bestowed to the elderly. Collecting paper, meanwhile, enters as a three-year-old by comparison—walking, talking, and toilet trained but decades away from full development and maturity.

Nearly 5,000 years ago, around 3000 BC, the Egyptians developed the use of papyrus, which would provide the origin of both the material and the term "paper." The reedy water plant was said to have thrived along the banks of the Nile River and in the marshes of Egypt, Palestine, and the entire Persian Gulf. Using crisscrossed strips of the plant with the water pressed out, Egyptians recorded the deeds of their times in scrolls that remain amazingly durable today. Of course, it should be noted that the papyrus scrolls were buried in the tombs of the great and mighty and not merely collected by the wise but meek.

Parchment paper first appeared around 190 BC. It was somewhat of an improvement as a recording archive, but it was kept only for its ability to document rules, regulations, and ownership.

A type of rag and pulp paper was fairly common during the early days of the English

colonies in America. It was this availability, in part, that led to the surge of colonial newspapers filled with the "freshest Advices both Foreign and Domestick" in major eastern cities. One cultured and refined citizen in colonial Williamsburg, John Custis, was said to have grumbled at the height of rag-paper popularity in the late 18th century, "I never

The Pennsylvania Gazette *newspaper, 1747,
printed by Benjamin Franklin. Photo courtesy of
Swann Galleries, Inc.*

have had any news papers in my life nor ever desire any. I do not regard who has lost a Spaniell bitch, who has died of the pox, and such stuff as' Gazettes are stuff'd with.''

But it was exactly that stuff in broadside and four-page tabloid weeklies that did so well in the days prior to the American Revolution. They often filled their front pages with major "foreign and domestick" news and with types of notices and advertisements inside. They were praised, damned, and passed around, but hardly collected as historical records of the time. Many of these newspapers survived because of the hardy nature of the paper they were printed on. Today they are treasured domestic documents of colonial life.

Two paper mills, one in Kentucky and one in Pennsylvania, "supplied much of the paper used in western Pennsylvania, Kentucky, Ohio, Indiana, Illinois, and even Missouri" following the Revolutionary War and into the early 19th century, according to Dard

Massachusetts Spy *newspaper, 1776, engraved masthead by Paul Revere. Photo courtesy of Swann Galleries, Inc.*

Hunter in *Papermaking: The History and Technique of an Ancient Craft.* Adds Hunter, "Both establishments played a very considerable part in the opening of the West."

While paper became more plentiful in a growing country that needed it more than ever, the quality—in terms of durability—declined as producers increasingly used wood pulp in their paper. Things got even worse at the onset of the Civil War, as demand outstripped even the lesser-quality paper supply. Meanwhile, "The paper available in southern states during the Civil War was of even poorer quality," according to Joe Nickell, writing in *Pen, Ink and Evidence.* "Wood pulp was at a premium, and such substitutes as cornhusks had to be found. It produced a paper so thin and fragile that today it rapidly crumbles and deteriorates unless it is kept under careful conditions, including the proper degree of temperature and humidity."

THE BEGINNINGS OF PAPER COLLECTING

Even so, it was under those circumstances in the Confederacy during the Civil War that there emerged one of the first serious, somewhat organized collectors of paper memorabilia. Jonathan Mayer was a minor clerk in the Confederate War Office in Richmond when he secretly began assembling what many would come to consider the world's largest, most complete collection of Civil War autographs and related material. As an aide to the Adjutant General, Mayer was in a position to view a vast array of military material as it came across his desk. When a letters or documents were doomed to be discarded and destroyed, Mayer removed the prized signatures and assembled them in a box. Had it not been for Mayer—one of America's earliest autograph collectors—the signatures of many Confederate military leaders would never have survived the ravages of the war.

When Richmond fell in 1865, as legend has it, Mayer fled with his precious collection of Civil War paper, but in too big of a hurry to stop for his clothing and personal belongings. Mayer died in 1919, and the collection remained in obscurity until it was discovered in storage nearly a century after it had been "rescued" from Richmond by a pioneer collector.

Following the Civil War, a number of collectors followed the Mayer method of clipping signatures from the vast number of North and South Civil War documents. While this succeeded in preserving many signatures which would have been otherwise lost to history, it parted the names forever from the documents they endorsed.

While autograph collectors during and right after the Civil War were rare, another type of collection that developed during that same period proved to be fairly widespread—trading cards. Early in the war, Louis Prang and his company had prospered by selling patriotic prints, maps, and covers. In 1863, Prang published a series of album cards picturing American birds. The boon for Prang

and other printers was that the cards were sold in sets with the express purpose of being collected and displayed in hardcover albums which Prang also provided.

"This specialty did not originate with Prang," points out Robert Jay in the absorbing book *The Trade Card in 19th Century America.* "Several other British and American lithographers were by the 1860s also beginning to produce such cards for this increasingly popular 19th-century hobby. However, more than any other other major American lithographer, Prang came to specialize in this aspect of the printing trade." There is every evidence, however, that these cards (postage stamps not withstanding) were one of the first paper collectibles to be acquired and assembled in an organized manner.

Beyond the clipping of Civil War signatures and the gathering of Prang cards in albums, there was a great Victorian fascination with accumulations of calling cards. During the late 18th century, proper young ladies were taught to maintain scrapbooks by pasting worthy verses and refined drawings

Late 19th-century promotion for Prang's Christmas cards.

Trade card, Tetlow Manufacturing Co., 1893, Philadelphia.

onto the blank pages of bound books. However, with the onset of the calling card in the second half of 19th century, scrapbooks became the hobby of men, women, and children. By the end of the 1860s, all manner of paper relating to Victorian life—beyond Prang and company's delightful cards—was being collected and pasted.

"The middle-class miss had little enough to do," notes Maurice Rickards reflecting on the era in *Collecting Printed Ephemera.* "Music, drawing, needlework, and the scrapbook were her chief creative outlets—and the scrapbook, we suspect, came easiest . . . With scissors and paste and a handful of printed oddments she composed an unwitting montage of her time. The album later accommodated the die-cut scraps of the chromolitho trade, and the albums themselves finally took charge—along with the Bible and the photograph album—of everyone's parlor table.

The typical scrapbook of the 1880s would contain shiny embossed scraps produced in Germany, a confirmation announcement made with silvered lace paper, artificial flowers, paper animals of various sizes, and the undaunted calling card.

In 1892, in the book *Our Deportment,* John Young detailed some of the elaborate ceremony involving the cards: "A person may make a card serve the purpose of a call, and it may either be sent in an envelope, by messenger or left in person. If left in person, one corner should be turned down. To indicate that the call is made on all or several members of the family, the card for the lady of the house is folded in the middle. If guests are visiting at the house, a card is left for each guest. To return a call made in person with a card enclosed in an envelope is an intimation that visiting between the parties is ended." Small wonder that Victorians jammed scores of visiting cards into individual albums which were sold specifically for that purpose.

On the wings of the calling card and the fascination with scraps of paper was also carried the trade card. Trade cards were similar hand-sized advertisements for the most popular products of the day. Usually printed in color, they too were eagerly stuffed into albums. One of the leaders in trade card use with Clark's O.N.T. Thread. "The thread companies were among the first to begin nationwide distribution of trade cards, and the use of children in narrative situations was frequent in the multitude of cards issued in the latter years of the century," Jay explains. These cards were "intended to be saved and collected in the family card album precisely because of the endearing genre quality of the image."

Another innovator was Lydia Pinkham, the 19th-century version of Dear Abby. Pinkham's Vegetable Compound and other products were directed specifically to women, and she encouraged them to write to her with their personal problems. Often her trade cards said explicitly "Put this in your album." Women who wrote to Pinkham would invari-

A-HEAD OF ALL OF THEM.

Clark's O.N.T. Thread advertising trade card, late 19th century.

ably get a personal reply, even into the 1890s, and all was well until a curious magazine journalist working for *Ladies Home Journal* discovered that Mrs. Pinkham had died in 1883, although her prose and products continued on for years to come.

By the end of the 19th century, magazines had become the favorite of advertisers, and trade cards dropped from use almost overnight. While magazines enjoyed soaring readership at the turn of the century, they left a collecting void that trade cards had fulfilled.

When postcards at last appeared on the market of the sparkling new 20th century, they were aimed, at least in part, at the same type of collector who had been so attracted to the trading cards of the past. Marian Klamkin wrote in the 1981 volume *Collectibles* that postcards were so collectible then because they were "originally published for collectors" and were thus a natural hobby the second time around. When first produced in the early 1900s, "they were collected in fancy albums and used to cover lampshades, screens, and wastebaskets. Many cards were produced in series and sets, and the picture postcard also became the medium on which manufacturers and retailers could advertise their wares for very little investment."

Postcards were the perfect vehicle for artists like Richard Felton Outcault, who gave the country great pioneer comic strips like "The Yellow Kid" and "Buster Brown" before an equally dazzling career in magazine and postcard advertising. Besides advertising, cards were issued and dutifully collected "for every special occasion, every holiday, and to appeal to people of every age and personality," concluded Klamkin. "Not a city or town existed that didn't have its Main Street recorded for posterity and picture postcards sold at the local drugstore."

The glory days of the postcard and collecting them had largely ended by the beginning of World War I, partly because greeting cards had caught on with the public and would become the next method for written and mailed communication. Little in the way of extensive paper collecting developed in the years that followed, certainly nothing with the national appeal of trading cards or postcards.

EARLY RESOURCES AND COLLECTING TRENDS

In 1946 Carl W. Drepperd published the *First Reader for Antique Collectors* in which he discussed collecting engravings, lithographs, and magazine drawings from early magazines, including the *Quilting Party,* which had appeared in various forms during the 19th century.

Drepperd made his strongest paper collectibles case, however, for lithographs. "Many antiques shops have a few Currier & Ives and lithographs by other American print makers on hand," he pointed out. "But shopping for lithographs in general antiques shops sometimes leaves much to be desired in terms of results. Go to the print shops dealing in old pictures and you'll be in a sort of print collector's paradise. Also, you'll be buying where expert knowledge of supply and demand stabilizes prices." History does not record how many people took Drepperd's advice and went off to "lithograph paradise."

William Paul Bricker put the business of paper collectibles into focus in a much broader way in 1951 with *The Complete Book of Collecting Hobbies.* It was still a time when some thought it was necessary to tell others what to collect.

Bricker's ideas for people then included playing cards, newspaper clippings, book matches, menus, and greeting cards. In singling out greeting cards, he reviewed their history, which extended back to Prang and the mid-19th century, but he was more interested in what was happening then. "Collectors mount these cards in albums, the same as snapshots and postcards," Bricker explained. "But you can also put them in a filing box. Some shops carry old-time greeting cards but your best bet is to read the ads in one of the collector's magazines." The book also gave honorable mention to circus and theatrical paper, calling cards, and labels.

"Winter Morning in the Country," 19th-century Currier & Ives lithograph.

Victorian calling cards, advertising fans, and cardboard souvenirs with printed advertisements were touted in 1965 by Katherine Morrison McClinton in *The Complete Book of Small Antiques Collecting.* "All these colorful relics of the past are collectible today," said McClinton. "They are found in old trunks, old scrapbooks and for sale at secondhand shops and at antiques shows. We can hardly call them antiques, yet they are as old as many other articles now passed on antiques, and since they are no longer used, they become curiosities and even rarities." Perhaps she was one of the first to really make a point about the relativity of age and availability in terms of paper "antiques."

Other books of the 1960s gave a hurried look to the usual greeting cards, playing cards, trade cards, lithographs, and circus papers. They also made passing reference to silhouettes, maps, historic wallpaper, trade catalogs, dime novels, and collecting autographs—which was well beyond the Civil War clipping-signature stage.

"Although great institutions may be taking the place of (autograph) collectors of unlimited means, the cultural benefit of the widespread increase in the number of collectors must not be overlooked," confided Gordon Banks in the *Concise Encyclopedia of American Antiques* in 1965. He accurately foresaw "more collectors than ever before . . . and a healthy trend toward books, articles, private studies and other evidence of scholarship."

Times have certainly changed. Paper collectors are no longer looked upon as elite hobbyists who pass their retirement years by filling scrapbooks. There are no longer any prescribed areas of collecting for the chosen few. Anyone is welcome to acquire what attracts them. And no bit of paper scrap is any longer considered unworthy. "As with other collectibles, the ultimate choice remains in the hands of the collector—whatever piques one's interest or strikes one's fancy or both," concluded Demaris Smith in *Preserving Your Paper Collectibles* in 1989. "What is treasure

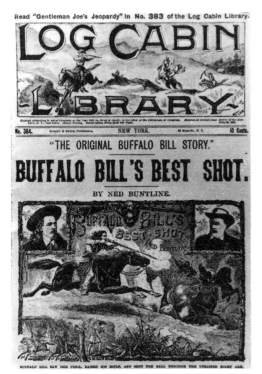

Dime novels of the 1890s popularized the Old West, especially with tales of Buffalo Bill.

to one person may be trash to another, but that should not diminish its collectible value. Age is not necessarily a factor. Items of the 1930s, 1940s, and 1950s are being rediscovered."

Browse through a stack of magazines on antiques from the 1960s and 1970s and you'll get the idea that paper of the past was not that much in demand. A 1963 issue of *The Antiques Journal* featured wanted ads for cartoons or original illustrations, books, and stamps, but overwhelmingly "wants" were for furniture, china, paisley shawls, and dolls.

Interestingly, during the entire year of 1963, the antiques monthly *Spinning Wheel* carried only one article on paper collectibles. It dealt with souvenir spoons and postcards. *Spinning Wheel* in 1967 carried classified ads for "anything printed or written" on early California, from the Gold Rush to Wells Fargo. There were also requests for presidential letters and documents, military commis-

sion papers before 1800, sports magazines, and trade cards. Ads also sought comic books, pulp magazines, and auto repair manuals published before 1940. But, comparatively, the vast number were again mainstream ads for jewelry, china, and general antiques. In 1970 an issue of *The Western Collector* included classified ads which sought original drawings, postcards, and color lithograph prints, but paper generally was given little attention.

In 1972 one of the first books devoted entirely to paper collectibles appeared on the market. *The Official Guide to Paper Americana* by Hal Cohen listed only four general-interest publications in the entire country dealing with antiques and collectibles. The book mentioned that a mint condition first edition of *Action Comics* was valued at $350, and war gum trading cards from the 1930s and 1940s brought anywhere from 10¢ to $1.50 each.

Looking back from the 1990s, it is strange to note that the full-length book did not include photographs, sports memorabilia, World War II posters or other World War II material, entertainment material other than movies, nor magazines. Dime novels, however, were listed. There was nothing on some of today's major categories of collecting such as television, transportation, and 20th-century advertising.

Even in an age when everything is thrown away, everything is also being sought out and collected. Magazines, checks, programs, tickets, membership cards, photographs, colorfully printed paper bags, and political campaign folders that all were once tossed away are now—by some—carefully tucked away. A few years ago the Collectors Connection and Registry conducted a random telephone survey of 1,000 households. They found that a full 75 percent of the people surveyed collected something. And even in the non-collector households, nearly everyone contacted had something among their personal belongings they considered quite collectible in today's market.

We are a nation of collectors. There are no limits as to experience, what our ancestors collected, or even personal taste. Like it or not, we are at last on our way to a new realization of our paper past. The novice is beginning to learn.

Eugene O'Neill wrote in *Long Day's Journey Into Night,* "The past is the present, isn't it? It's the future too." At this point in time, so much of the past of future collectibles remains to be discovered.

CHAPTER TWO

Preparing for Paper Paradise

*"You've got to be careful if you don't know where
you're going, because you might not get there."*
—*Yogi Berra*

In recent years, the national daily newspaper *USA Today* published a poll showing two-thirds of those surveyed would live somewhere in the past if they had a choice. Of course, sometime in the future, you may be able to have it both ways.

About the same time the poll results were published, a New York cable television company announced plans to set up a 100-channel system that could be eventually expanded to 1,000 or more channels. One channel was being reserved just for *Time Magazine.*

It would seem to be just a matter of time before you can punch up a channel devoted to your favorite category of paper collectibles. Or what about a live view of various paper shows about the country? Somewhere in the future, we may well be surrounded by the past from multichannel viewing to ultra-specialized reading.

MAGAZINES, NEWSLETTERS, AND PERIODICALS

Information, the experts say, will double in the world every ten years. This may also mean that the number of experts will also double in that span of time. (Or will some of the ones we already have simply double in size?) The point for collectors of paper memorabilia is that information is doubling just as the technology for finding it, storing it, and studying it is exploding. Already what is available to the average collector is staggering.

Take trading cards. There was a point in the late 1980s when little information on trading cards was readily available to the public on a regular basis. This was particularly true when compared to the wealth of newspaper-magazine choices on hand for sports cards collectors. But things slowly began to change.

No. 7 Tracy Questions the Gardener   No. 8 Pat Shadows a Suspect   No. 10 Big Boy Elimina

Dick Tracy trading cards, 1930s, issued by Walter Johnson Candy Co. Photo courtesy of Hake's Americana & Collectibles.

First, sports cards publications added sections on trading non-sports cards. Next, there were entire trading card magazines that went from specialized subscriber readership to thriving newsstand sales, and into the 1990s there were at least four such publications going strong.

Meanwhile the editorial coverage expanded from just cards and sets to unopened packages, uncut sheets, promotional posters, and even display boxes. Not every paper category will expand as quickly and as decisively as trading cards, but the potential is clear.

National

There are enough daily, weekend, and weekly newspapers for 177 million Americans according to the American Newspaper Publishers Association. That amounts to more than 10,000 different newspapers published for general readership and thousands more for special interests, including collectors.

Nobody, but nobody, has a complete list of all the antiques and collectibles publica-

JUNE 1967 — 55 cents

Treasure of the Spanish Main (page 14)

Spinning Wheel *antiques magazine, June 1967.*

tions now available. I would estimate between 200 and 300 now exist, counting the various regional periodicals which regularly pop to the surface. Have you ever heard of the *Indiana Antique Buyer* or even seen it on a list of publications? You wouldn't likely run into it unless you frequent shops and malls in the Hoosier state, yet it serves thousands of residents and travelers. The point is that the country is full of similar publications which are not only flourishing but also providing an important service to the reader.

Then there are publications dealing specifically with paper collectibles. Among them:

The Ephemera News, a newsletter published by the Ephemera Society of America, PO Box 37, Schoarie, NY 12157, (518) 295-7978.

Grandma's Trunk, a newsletter on trade cards, valentines, rewards of merit, etc. It is available from PO Box 404, Northport, MI 49670, (616) 386-5351.

Paper Pile Quarterly, a booklet on many aspects of paper available from PO Box 337, San Anselmo, CA 94979.

Paper and Advertising Collector (PAC), newspaper published by the National Association of Paper and Advertising Collectors, PO Box 500, Mount Joy, PA 17552, (717) 653-4300.

Paper Collectors' Marketplace (PCM), PO Box 128, Scandinavia, WI 54977, (715) 467-2379. (Each monthly issue contains 96–120 pages of information, articles, advertisements, and classifieds. I would highly recommend it.)

The World Press Review says there are more than 11,000 different magazines published in the United States, which sounds impressive, but the better-positioned *MagazineWeek* says there are more than 24,000. And that is, as they say in the exploding information age, just the beginning. Don Nicholas, the editor of *MagazineWeek,* has said in published comments, "If there are 24,000 magazines today, I would fully expect that in ten years there will be 48,000. As magazines go paperless, it's going to explode."

Paperless magazines, i.e., those online on computer networks, will be much easier to produce and will be cost effective enough to target a very small but dedicated audience, like collectors of 20th-century Halloween postcards, for example. "I'm a firm believer that paper magazines will become antiques," adds Nicholas. "And distinctions between magazines, books, and newspapers are going to blur."

Here is a double-stagger for the paper collector. First, common paper publications as we know them may be disappearing. I am reminded of Tom Heberlein's comments in 1993. The University of Wisconsin-Madison sociologist suggested that by the year 2027 hunters will be extinct. Professor Heberlein presented the case that due to the decline of deer and other wild animals, relative lack of interest by youngsters, and changing public opinion, the activity would disappear. The situation is interesting. If you were attracted to the paper memorabilia related to hunting, what would you begin saving before it slowly vanished? Where would you begin? Could it be that many varieties of paper magazines will soon become an endangered species?

Second, if Nicholas and others are correct, the scope of specialized coverage of collecting categories will increase a thousandfold. As a result, collectors of paper may find themselves in a very unique relationship in the future, benefiting from the vast diversity of the information age, on the one hand, and collecting artifacts on the paper age that preceded it.

Today general antiques and collectibles publications reflect a significant national interest in paper collectibles. The following recommended publications are not entirely dedicated to paper, but typically offer considerable editorial coverage and advertising on that subject:

Today's Collector, 700 E. State St., Iola, WI 54990, (800) 258-0929 (show calendar in every monthly issue).

Collectors News, PO Box 156, Grundy Center, IA 50638, (319) 824-6981 or 800-352-8039 (show calendar in every monthly issue).

Antique Trader, PO Box 1050, Dubuque, IA 52001, (319) 588-2073 or 800-334-7165 (show calendar in every weekly issue).

Antique Week, PO Box 90, Knightstown, IN 46148, (317) 345-5133 or 800-876-5133 (show calendar in every weekly issue).

Antiques & Collecting Hobbies, 1006 S. Michigan Ave., Chicago, IL 60605, (312) 939-4767 (show calendar in every monthly issue).

The western
COLLECTOR
VOLUME VIII   NUMBER 5   MAY 1970

Spanish Colonial Material
James F. Shafer, II, discusses earthenware jars, beads and drinking bottles from the Spanish Colonial Period in the New World.

Pioneer for Today's Collector

WESTERN COLLECTOR IS THE OFFICIAL VOICE OF THE FEDERATION OF HISTORICAL BOTTLE CLUBS

The Western Collector *collectibles magazine, May 1970.*

Here, also are some leading regional publications which are laden with general information and events in various parts of the country:

East

Brimfield Antique Guide, RR1, Route 20, Brimfield, MA 01010, (413) 245-9329.

Mid Atlantic Antiques Magazine, PO Box 908, Henderson, NC 27536, (919) 492-4001.

Treasure Chest, 253 W. 72 St., #211A, New York, NY 10013, (212) 496-2234.

Renninger's Antique Guide, PO Box 495, Lafayette Hill, PA 19444, (215) 828-4614.

Midwest

Antique Collector and Auction Guide, PO Box 38, Salem, OH 44460, (216) 337-3419.

Buckeye Marketeer, PO Box 954, Westerville, OH 43081, (614) 895-9329.

Indiana Antique Buyer, PO Box 213, Silver Lake, IN 46982, (219) 982-7074.

The Collector, PO Box 158, Heyworth, IL 61745, (309) 473-2466.

Yesteryear, PO Box 2, Princeton, WI 54968, (414) 787-4808.

South

Antique Shoppe, 12055 Southeast Highway 441, Belleview, FL 32620, 800-847-1740.

Antique Gazette, Suite 106, 6949 Charlotte Pike, Nashville, TN 37209, (615) 352-0941.

Antique Traveler, PO Box 656, Mineola, TX 75773, 800-446-3588.

Southeastern Antiques & Collectibles Monthly, PO Box 730, Macon, GA 31202, (912) 742-8614.

West

Arizona Antique News, PO Box 26536, Phoenix, AZ 85068, (602) 943-9137.

Antiques Today, 977 Lehigh Circle, Carson City, NV 89705, (702) 267-4600.

Art, Antiques & Collectibles, PO Box 5858, Santa Rosa, CA 95402, (707) 769-9916.

Antiques & Collectibles, PO Drawer 1565, El Cajon, CA 92022, (619) 593-2925.

BOOKS

Today, in contrast to most of the rest of the 20th century, there are entire books or price guides on specialized fields of paper collectibles that were not even mentioned a few generations ago in the broadest-based books of the day. For the paper generalist, these books may be available in book stores or libraries:

Warman's Paper by Norman Martinus and Harry Rinker, Wallace-Homestead, 1994, a paper ephemera price guide.

Collecting Paper by Gene Utz, Books Americana, 1993, a price guide.

Pen, Ink and Evidence by Joe Nickel, University of Kentucky Press, 1990.

Preserving Your Paper Collectibles by Demaris Smith, Betterway Publications, 1989.

Turning Paper to Gold by Joseph Lefontaine, Betterway Publications, 1988.

Collecting Printed Ephemera by Maurice Richards, Abbeville Press, 1988.

Official Price Guide to Paper Collectibles, 5th Edition, House of Collectibles, 1986.

The *U.S. Statistical Abstract* reports that a typical day sees 124 books published, including 22 on economics and 4 on art. There is one book on antiques and collectibles published nearly every day in the year.

In 1989, when hundreds of books were being published in the field annually, our small company, Antique and Collectible News Service (ACNS), began offering book reviews and lists of new book to publications around the country. We felt the service was needed, in part, because most publications simply could not handle the volume of new arrivals on the market. Many good books were just getting stacked in a corner. On the other hand, many publishers—especially those on a limited budget—could not afford to send review copies to the growing number of antiques and collectibles publications nationwide.

Additionally, few editors had the time to even casually read and record the 30 to 40 books filling the market each month. As a result, most readers had no real idea of what books were available on their specific area of interest.

The monthly reviews and the accompanying "Good Reeding" list proved to be highly successful. And book publishers were pleased because a central source of promotion was provided. Today, dozens of publications subscribe to the service, and readers everywhere—we estimate the number at over 700,000—can stay informed and up to date.

For the determined few who want to get beyond that, there are the major antiques and collectibles books publishers, most of which will provide a list or catalog at no charge upon written request. These include:

Books Americana, PO Box 2336, Florence, AL 35630. Catalog includes about 28 new and backlist titles.

Collector Books, PO Box 3009, Paducah, KY 42002. Seasonal catalog includes 190 titles, additional order booklet includes 375–400 titles plus backlists, including books from other publishers.

Dover Publications, 31 East 2nd St., Mineola, NY 11505. Catalog lists over 300 books, including reprints of old retail catalogs.

L-W Book Sales, PO Box 69, Gas City, IN 46933. Order booklet offers 600 titles, including those from other publishers and backlist.

Schiffer Publishing, 77 Lower Valley Rd., Rt. 372, Atglen, PA 19310. Seasonal catalog with backlist includes about 420 Schiffer titles.

Wallace-Homestead, One Chilton Way, Radnor, PA 19089. Biannual catalog of about 120 current and backlist Wallace-Homestead and Warmon titles.

VIDEOS

And last, but not least, there are videos, which are rapidly becoming specialized.

Some years ago ACNS purchased a VCR for office use and I wondered aloud if the expense would ever be justified. I began a file on advertisements, brochures, and letters which mentioned videos on antiques and collectibles. In a year it was pretty full; now it is inevitable that new videos be added to the book review lists.

Advision currently offers 200 different titles on collecting in areas such as postcards, paper money, and baseball cards. A free listing of titles is available from Advison, 3100 Arrowwood Lane, Boulder, CO 80303-2419. The American Antique Graphics Society, meanwhile, offers at a modest cost a video of the items in their paper collectibles auctions. Write to 5185 Windfall Road, Medina, Ohio 44256.

As to what information is available to the collector of paper antiques and collectibles, I would point to the famous first line of Dr. Benjamin Spock in the classic *Baby and Child Care* book: "You know more than you think you do."

CHAPTER THREE

Pricing Factors for Paper Collectibles

"The true, strong and sound mind is the mind that can embrace equally great things and small."
—*Samuel Johnson*

Many years ago I worked for a boss who was a true jerk. This boss was probably not unlike those many of you have encountered and endured from time to time, except this one accidentally provided me with quite a windfall of paper collectibles.

It was major remodeling time at the newspaper where I worked, and everything had to go in order to make room for new furnishings and hardware. As editor, I had inherited quite a stack of old wire-service photographs which dated back to the early 1960s. In the '60s the pictures, sometimes called silver prints, had a hard glossy finish and never faded or wilted.

To me the old pictures were good resources for our files. But to Mr. Wizard they were clutter. The architects and the owners had plans, and these "dumpy" black-and-white photographs would not be part of the wave of the future. Quietly I cleaned them all out, but I ignored orders to simply trash them. Much like the kid who has found a stray dog, I brought them home.

Over the next dozen or so years, I would occasionally paw through the group of about 200 photographs, but I honestly never thought they held any real interest for the outside world. One day reality struck. While researching an article on photographs, I ran across a catalog from prestigious Swann Galleries in New York City. Among the cur-

rent listings they had included a few lots of—sorry Mr. Wizard—wire-service photos from the 1960s. Shortly afterwards I ran across a transaction in another part of the country in which four wire photos relating to the Kennedy assassination sold for a total of $250.

All this is not to say I quit my day job and

Neil Armstrong, astronaut on the moon, 1969 silver print. Photo courtesy of Swann Galleries, Inc.

John F. Kennedy and daughter Caroline, July 1963, wire service photo.

moved to the South Seas. Prices always vary and there are always related costs in such transactions, or even in accepting wholesale prices from an enterprising dealer. Still, these old photos will eventually realize a tidy sum. Maybe I'll send Boss Numbskull a card.

There are four significant points to consider in judging prices on paper collectibles: scarcity, durability, investment return, and context.

SCARCITY

It is not necessarily age, but desirability and scarcity that most often affect pricing of paper collectibles. A lot of paper collectibles which were once plentiful become nonexistent after 20 or 30 years. As a civilization, we produce more paper than ever before in history, but we also throw away more, too.

In 1993 a major news network feature disclosed a study which found that over 50 percent of the material in landfills was not disposable diapers, garbage, or grass clippings, but plain old paper—newspapers, magazines, junk mail, grocery sacks, and so forth. (Interestingly enough, the researchers found 30-year-old newspapers that were remarkably well preserved and readable.)

Of the 187,000 tons of paper used each day in this country—from paper napkins to toilet tissue—about 98 percent is disposed of within a few months. Concerning the best of the rest, another 83 cubic feet of books, films, letters, and documents are gathered up by the National Archives in Washington each day. According to Tom Parker, the author of *In One Day,* "That's about six steamer trunks of stuff added to the nation's attic" at the end of every evening. Meanwhile, the Smithsonian Institution adds an additional 2,700 things to its collections each and every day, much of which is part of America's legacy of paper collectibles.

If and when paper from fast-food restaurants becomes a really worthwhile collectible, it will take future generations quite some time to accumulate because the stuff from Wendy's, Burger King, and McDonald's gets pitched just about as quickly as the food is consumed.

On a personal note, my mother was one of the models used for the Morton Salt girl in the 1920s. As a result, I have spent some time gathering materials with the image of the young girl that matches some of the original artwork in my possession. The 1921 ink blotter may have been listed in a price guide at $5, but I would have gladly paid twice that amount. Such a find could (and sometimes does) involve months of searching shops, making telephone calls, and writing letters.

DURABILITY

Certain subjects have a topical vitality that keeps them popular and well-priced for generations. Disney, Barbie, and Elvis memorabilia have thrived in the second half of the 20th century and probably will continue to do well for some time to come. Americans buy 38,000 Barbie and Barbie-related dolls every day. They also spend $125,000 on Elvis merchandise and entertainment daily. The enterprises of The King make more money now than they did when the singer was alive. You could go back further in time and consider paper material related to Abraham Lincoln or even Babe Ruth has having that same eternal durability with collectors.

Of course, texture of the paper itself has to be durable so that it does not crumble, especially when the best safeguards are taken. But the durability of content is highly important. My favorite example is *The Adventures of Mickey Mouse, Book 1,* since I had a secondhand copy of one as a child. In 1993, Swann Galleries sold an original cloth version issued by the David McKay Company in 1931. Swann estimated it to be worth between $800 and $1,200; it eventually brought $2,200.

Another factor influencing the durability of topics are price guides. Is it a known entity listed in the major price guides, or is it a

The Adventures of Mickey Mouse, *1931, David McKay Co. Photo courtesy of Hake's Americana & Collectibles.*

freaky thing just written up in the local newspaper? Value guides, of course, come with their own controversy. Some people question whether they reflect the prices of the marketplace or, indeed, affect the marketplace with their own interpretation of what values should be. One theory proposes that if Mary Sunshine has an exceptional collection of paper valentines and puts a semi-fictional price guide together, in doing so she builds the value of her own collection tremendously. It can and does happen. But for the most part, considering the hundreds of value guides issued annually by reliable authors and publishing companies, it is mostly just grumbling from would-bes and wanna-bes.

For one thing, like it or not, we live in the golden age of information. There are newsletters, auction catalogs, magazines, tabloids, books, videos, shows, thousands of shops, and even computer networks that offer prices. Given such a climate, it would be impossible to manipulate the market for long.

A few years ago my wife and I put together a price guide on trading cards (i.e., Batman, TV shows, Elvis, World War II, birds and animals, and movie stars). At the time there were four nationally distributed magazines which were totally committed to prices of trading cards. Moreover, there were at least a dozen more magazines with limited listings of trading cards. In short, the market prices, with some slight variation, were pretty well established. The book simply put a great deal of the information into a single volume along with prices from scores of mail-order, catalog, auction, and advertised sources. It covered more than 100 years of trading card production in a single volume and was highly successful.

By and large, price guides in the field of antiques and collectibles perform a substantial service in guiding both the buyer and the seller. They are not the final word—unlike a catalog. They are merely one of the tools the wise collector keeps in the handy toolbox.

Price guides do have a role in maintaining durability of paper collectibles. People everywhere become aware of what an item is and the relative value of it, and that reference surely makes interest in it that much more durable.

INVESTMENT RETURN

It is not unreasonable to consider paper collectibles an investment; and, therefore, it is fair to take that somewhat into account in considering prices. If you spend $500 on golfing, all you can really expect in return is a good time. If you invest that amount in paper collectibles, you could expect to recover some of it some day, and maybe even realize a profit. All this may not equal a killing in the stock market, but to purchase a prized paper artifact, view and enjoy it over the years, and finally sell it for a higher price than you paid is not a bad deal either.

A key point to investing in paper is realizing that 10 to 15 years from now the potential buyers for your material will be totally unlike any we have seen thus far. They will be far more informed, more resourceful, and more adaptable than ever before in history. There will also be more collectors out there, and they will have more money to spend, too. These "super buyers" will be armed with videos, computers, electronic books and magazines, and hundreds of price guides.

As the ranks of collectors increase, the number of professional dealers will also continue to increase, providing a network—even if still unofficial and unorganized—of available paper materials nationwide. Moreover, the diversity of collecting continues to grow. People collect postcards for the stamps, the postmarks of towns that no longer exist, the topics on the front, the publishers, the historical era, the region of the country, the sports-related content, advertising, cultures portrayed (including African-American), and many other reasons. These cross purposes of collecting add directly to the potential of your investment.

Bear in mind there are some downsides to investments in paper. For one thing, most material goes from the dealer to the customer and back again. This means that if you spend $100 on paper collectibles and are fortunate enough to double your money in five years, the $200 worth of paper will generally bring you only half that amount from the dealer who must allow for profit and expense. That could leave you with just the original investment of $100 and no profit. Some alternatives are selling directly to accomplished collectors, selling on consignment (this means basically putting your own price on material and paying the dealer a percentage of the sale), or becoming a dealer, in varying degrees, yourself.

The collector/investor turned dealer generally comes armed with advanced knowledge, obtained over the five years or so of holding material, and an awareness of potentially helpful individuals and organizations. The investment factor is a strong motivation for collecting paper, making it a big business as well as just a hobby. There two types of paper collectibles investments now available: *zero investing* and *progressive investing*.

Zero Investing

Zero investing means you paid little or nothing to acquire an item such as tickets, newspapers, magazines, trading cards, comic books, or a children's record album, to list only a few. Often zero investing provides relatively small amounts of profit since the initial amount itself is minor. However, this is not always the case. In 1956 Bubbles Inc. issued Elvis Presley gum cards to the public. One package with gum and a single card sold for 1¢, another package with five cards and gum sold for 5¢. There were ultimately 66 cards in the entire set, which means that an eager youngster could have spent $1 and pretty well rounded-up the whole set with cards to spare. In 1994 the single Elvis cards from 1956 were listed in leading price guides at around $9 each and the full sets were $530. Even by Wall Street standards that would not have been a bad "zero" investment.

Other lesser-impact examples are a paperback book, *Free Ride,* sold on the newsstands in 1957 for 25¢ and now collectible at

The Seven Year Itch *production photo with Marilyn Monroe, 1955. Photo courtesy of Hake's Americana & Collectibles.*

$4; a Walt Disney Golden Book featuring Zorro published in 1958 for 59¢ and now worth $18; a coloring book based on the TV show *Mackenzie's Raiders* originally sold for 29¢ in 1960 and goes currently for $30; *See* magazine from 1955 with Marilyn Monroe on the cover was issued at 15¢ per copy and is now a $35 collector's item; finally, the cover price of a program for the 1956 Indianapolis 500-mile race was 50¢ and to acquire one today would take about $28.

Progressive Investing

Progressive investing involves buying paper materials which already have some collector value but have the potential over time to be worth even more. In 1984 a buyer purchased an autographed manuscript of Albert Einstein's 1929 paper on the Unified Field Theory for $38,500. In 1994 the same manuscript sold at Swann Galleries in New York City for more than $100,000. Here's another example. Using the *Official Price Guide To Paper Collectibles* in 1985, the wise collector/ shopper could have made the following purchases of trading card sets in very good condition: America Salutes the FBI-Heroes of the Law from 1949 for $72; American Indian Chiefs from 1888 for $225; U.S. Presidents from 1952 for $27; and the Bionic Woman set from 1976 for $8.25. Today the FBI set lists at $600, Indian Chiefs go for $1,100, U.S. Presidents are $165, and the Bionic Woman set is $30.

No fantastic return can be expected on the vast majority of paper collectibles. However, most experts we surveyed pointed out that it would not be unreasonable to expect good-quality paper items to double in value within about ten years—in other words, a growth of roughly ten percent annually. However, the keys are quality material, fine condition, and a fair purchase price. "Good is always going to be good," notes one leading dealer in the field. "But don't pay three times the going rate for a paper item and expect to get your money back. Enjoy it and save it for your grandchildren. Maybe they will eventually double the original investment for you."

CONTEXT

Perhaps the most far-reaching factor in the price of paper collectibles is the context—the purpose the item served when it was first created and what it meant to the people involved with it. It relates to the innate feeling of then and now.

In the mail-order *Shaker Catalog No. 19,* Scott DeWolf observed that a critical consideration is the way a collectible affected society, historically speaking. "Context can be difficult to gather as most dealers and collectors have not preserved the history of the pieces that have passed through their hands," DeWolf noted. "It is the astute person who attempts to capture the history or cultural significance of what he or she collects. By studying the context of artifacts, we are no longer simply accumulators of relics but rather social historians who are attempting to document a specific way of life and to understand an artifact in its terms, rather than ours; to understand an artifact's past as well as how that artifact continues to work in the present."

Many years ago while adding to a collection of old newspapers, I acquired a copy of the *Selma Federal Union.* The May 5, 1865, issue contains "Glorious News" about the end of the fighting in the Civil War, but what made it unique among most Civil War newspapers was that it was published by federal troops after they had seized a Confederate newspaper office in Selma, Alabama. The result was a newspaper filled with articles about the war's ending, funeral arrangements for President Lincoln, plus a bit of propaganda for the local citizens. Both the text and the context, in this case, go toward making this particular *Selma Federal Union* worth two or three times more than the average Civil War newspaper.

Sometimes the importance of context slips by even the best of observers. Take the tale of the Cardiff giant—a 10-foot 4½-inch, 2,990-pound giant reportedly unearthed near Syracuse, New York, in 1869. As it turned out, the Cardiff giant was one of the biggest hoaxes of the 19th century, but for a time, the whole country bought the story. Actually the scheme of a tobacco farmer, the giant was carved by two sculptors from a five-ton block of gypsum. Sulfuric acid was added for aging purposes and about a year later the giant was "discovered" under five feet of earth.

By the end of 1869, the hoax had been pretty much revealed, but the stone giant endured and today it is displayed in the Farmers' Museum at Cooperstown, New York, under the administration of the New York State Historical Association. A second giant was created by the fabled P.T. Barnum after he was rebuffed in his attempts to purchase the Cardiff giant.

In the spring of 1993, Swann Galleries staged a major ephemera auction which in-

Broadside poster for the Great Cardiff Giant, 1869, Albany, New York. Photo courtesy of Swann Galleries, Inc.

cluded a small broadside poster promoting the Great Cardiff Giant and urging the public to view it at the Geological Hall in Albany. Swann estimated the poster would bring $100 to $150. It actually brought $247 and, considering the background and context, someone still got a real bargain.

Much of context value can be purely generational. Test yourself. What was fun when you were, say, ten years old—the advertisements, restaurants, toys, entertainment, radio-TV shows, comic books, greeting cards, and record albums you enjoyed? On the other hand, what made a lifetime impression?

When I was a child, the grim days of World War II were still a part of my life. My father never marched off to war, he was beyond the age limit. Instead, he devoted his war effort to being an air-raid warden. Some of my earliest memories are of the blackouts and my father, with flashlight and white-painted steel helmet, going out into the night as the sirens wailed. Sometimes my mother and I could see him from our second-story apartment window as he moved slowly about the streets, a speck of light in the darkness. Today I still have his Air Raid Warden card issued by the Civil Defense Corps. He was quite proud of it then, and I am quite proud of it today.

Of course, adults with comfortable incomes seek to buy back the glory days of their childhood by finding things similar to what impressed them as youngsters. This has long been true of toys. It was also instrumental in

fueling the baseball card craze and has a bearing on paper collectibles.

Where are those valentines, trading cards, movie star photos, travel postcards, *TV Guides,* playing cards, comic books, menus, and membership cards from your past? That type of context, or childhood factor, "can become a very emotional thing," explains Anthony Curtis, the noted author of over 160 worldwide guides on antiques and collectibles. "When it becomes so intertwined with their childhood, money is totally secondary. People will pay anything." Curtis says this is especially true of people in their 40s and 50s who are finally motivated to seek out the things of their childhood. "First they'll call home and see if any of it is still there. Then they start hunting elsewhere."

Perhaps a "second cousin" to collectors of this type are those who seek out paper items related to their jobs. Nurses, doctors, lawyers, police officers, military leaders, school teachers, government workers, and airline personnel are some of the occupation-related fields to collect.

Beyond such considerations there is a natural collectibility about paper that figures into prices and values. Most paper from the past is readily identifiable, and a lot of it is even marked and dated. That makes it relatively easy to collect, and the person in New York will readily know what the person in Podunk is talking about.

Already communication about these collectibles spans the globe and will become even more widespread with increasing technology. Fax a copy of your favorite paper collectible to London, or better yet send a color TV transmission via computer network. You can even send the item itself across the country and have it delivered within 24 hours. With paper so identifiable, Fax-able, and movable, it stands as one of the most documentable antiques and collectibles in the entire world.

Ultimately, paper collectibles will lend themselves to increasing specialization—the wave of the future. Auctions and other outlets for collectors will center more and more on

Air raid warden card issued by Civil Defense Corps, early 1942.

one particular category. Specific paper will be offered at finely researched sales with well-educated buyers.

USE

Finally, pricing of paper collectibles also involves decorating considerations. In the antiques business, you learn fairly early that decorators can be a significant force in the marketplace, often beating collectors to the punch on attractive pieces. As decorating with collectibles moves to the forefront in homes and offices, people who have not even thought about collecting football programs or Coke display cards will be trying to visualize just how a bedroom bulletin board from the 1950s would have looked.

Decorating with collectible paper can be just as charming and creative as the owner wants it to be. The kitchen or snack areas of the home can be adorned with fast food restaurant stock certificates, posters, menus, wrappers, napkins, signs, and premiums. The bathroom mirror and sink can be lined with placards bearing products of the past—combs, aspirin, nail files, hair nets, laxatives. A work area can take on a cowboy atmosphere with black-and-white photo stills of old movies, arcade cards of cowboy stars, lobby cards, and small posters combined with toy pistols and a cowboy hat. Or it could become automobilia heaven with road maps, gasoline signs, product display cards typically found in service stations of prior decades, and gasoline credit cards.

The decorating trend now seems to favor focusing on a power corner featuring paper collectibles rather than having the items spread out over one or more rooms. Putting it all together adds to the intensity and interest. A Raggedy Ann and Andy corner might include dolls, books, magazine covers, advertisements, curtains, paper party products (including napkins and paper plates), greeting cards, board games, and puzzles. A kitchen corner can be compelling with cereal boxes, colorful oat containers, and soap boxes. A

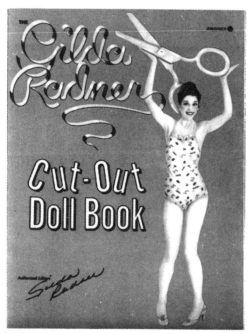

Gilda Radner paper doll book, 1979, Avon Books, 12 pages. Photo courtesy of Hake's Americana & Collectibles.

Gilda Radner paper doll, 1979, Avon Books, 12 pages. Photo courtesy of Hake's Americana & Collectibles.

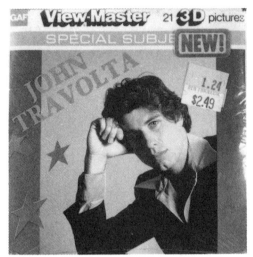

John Travolta View-Master reel envelope, 1979. Photo courtesy of Hake's Americana & Collectibles.

Hopalong Cassidy coloring book, ca. 1940, Abbot Publishing Co. Photo courtesy of Hake's Americana & Collectibles.

Victorian spot can be filled with 19th-century billheads, photographs, posters, and framed magazine covers. Aviation, advertising, Barbie, Garfield, banking, entertainment, and school days are all themes which could leap from the walls with the appropriate photos, postcards, ads, greeting cards, magazines, and specific objects.

Typically, bright, stark artwork usually works best in decorating—sports programs and posters in the activity room, fruit and vegetable crate labels in the kitchen, Star Wars packaged toys and trading cards in the bedroom, or Little Golden Books in neat stacks and framed along with corresponding stuffed toys for a child's room. Paper collectibles acquired for display may be bolder or somewhat more theme-related than those

simply intended to be part of more subtle collection. Always avoid direct sunlight in displaying, and to be especially protective, rotate the displays every few months or at least seasonally.

In the book *The Day America Told The Truth,* authors James Patterson and Peter Kim make a rather grim forecast on future childhood-related collecting based on vast research and a survey of thousands of Americans. "American children do not have the idealized youth of earlier generations— whether that even existed in fact or not, we believed that it did," they wrote in 1991. "The growing-up years of 11 to 16 have changed to the point that it's accurate to speak of the end of the childhood." It is hard to think there will be no equivalent of our Batman comic books, Gilda Radner paper dolls, Yukon King trading cards, Hopalong Cassidy coloring books, and John Travolta View-Master reels out there somewhere holding special memories for future generations.

CHAPTER FOUR

The Marketplace for Paper Collectibles

When you come to a fork in the road, take it.
—*Yogi Berra*

• •

The marketplace for paper collectibles can be as close as your closet or as far away as the other side of the world. It can also be everywhere in between. To begin with, most households are filled with paper products of various kinds and purposes, and various ages, but with two things in common: each is, of course, paper and it has somehow survived.

A couple I know prospered quite well in one large midwestern city by running small advertisements offering to clean out attics and garages for free. The deal was that in exchange for the cleaning and hauling, they got to keep everything—trash and treasure—that was unwanted by the owners. For them and their customers, it was a wonderful arrangement. Very simply put, those old attics and garages were the couple's marketplace and the currency they used was their own labor. To be sure, the busy pair eventually sold all kinds of antiques and collectibles to surrounding dealers, thereby realizing a cash profit.

COLLECTING BEGINS AT HOME

The marketplace starts right at the household where ordinary paper may have acquired treasured status to outsiders. It can therefore be the starting block of a fine new collection, or it can be used as your "currency" in exchange for some entirely different material. One good example is a photograph handed down for several generations of the

same family, much more as a simple keepsake than a treasured heirloom. After much research, the tiny 2½-by-3½-inch tintype of a young man in the late 1870s in a small town in New Mexico was sold at a major New York City auction gallery in 1994. As it turned out, it was only the second authenticated portrait of the notorious American outlaw Billy the Kid and it brought over $50,000 from a private collector.

Rain check for 1914 Indianapolis Motor Speedway 500-mile race.

So the tip is to start cleaning and checking, and then offer to do grandma's place, and Aunt Stella's, and so forth.

THE LOCAL MARKETPLACE

Garage sales are, for the most part, great fun because they represent the purest essence of searching for paper collectibles. Short of personally pawing around in people's households, the garage sale is the next best thing. Folks put everything imaginable out for sale (trust me—after 20 years I have seen one or two of everything) because they basically want to get rid of it. They expect to make a few dollars, but 99 percent know nothing of the value of paper collectibles and could really care less. Some experts will say it is alright to bargain down prices at garage sales because one-time-only sellers are inexperienced. I disagree. Pay these grass-roots sources what they ask if you find something nice. You will still likely take home a bargain and you will feel much better about yourself.

A few years ago a couple in London spotted two watercolors in some shabby frames at a flea market. The asking price was $3 complete with frames. But the couple cut a deal to by the pictures of wildflowers for $1.50 and the dealer could keep the frames. As it turned out, the watercolors of wildflowers and sandy dunes was by artist Andrew Nicholl, who died in 1886. Some months later, the same two watercolors sold at Sotheby's auction gallery for nearly $13,000. It was reported that the anonymous couple spent their profits on a visit to relatives in Australia.

Thousands upon thousands of garage and yard sales are held in the United States every single week (weather permitting), and there are bargains to be found at most of them. Here are some suggestions:

1. If you are looking for treasured paper collectibles, be there at the starting time or before, while all the obvious gems are still there.

2. Watch for old magazines and various other papers slipped within their pages.

3. Old cookbooks are nearly always stuffed with printed receipts, paper premiums, and colorful advertising folders.

4. Carefully check all the boxes of old toys for children's books, comic books, coloring books, and similar material. Often you have to settle for fairly used condition, but at the same token, you are generally paying only a fraction of the market value.

5. Watch for boxes containing assortments of items which may include black-and-white photographs, certificates, calendars, almanacs, or booklets for electrical appliances from the past.

6. Nearly every sale has a box of paperback books. Look for ones from the 1940s and 1950s in good condition.

7. Remember the hinterlands. As a rule of thumb, the further the town from a large city, the greater the chance of finding great collectibles.

And there are still other ways to expand the local marketplace. Many professional antiques and collectibles buyers move about, advertising in local newspapers that they are seeking to purchase items. The advertisements invite people to telephone a number and set up an appointment for the buyer to visit the home, inspect the items, and make an offer. The professional buyers then, in turn, sell the material either through an established auction or antiques mall. No doubt, this approach can reap some wonderful results, but as one veteran "circuit rider" explained, "Going into homes is really a business type of thing. It takes a great deal of time and travel to do properly. That, and all the paper work involved, is why malls and shops are such a popular alternative."

In the 1991 best-selling novel *Needful Things,* Stephen King wrote of a antiques shop which became an overnight success. But it was definitely not just another antiques shop. Eleven-year-old Brian Rusk learned it had "a little of everything, that's what a successful business is about, Brian." The paper collectible Brian acquired was an autographed 1956 Topps card of Sandy Koufax.

The boy paid only 85¢ for the item but found it wasn't such a bargain after all.

Needful Things aside, the adventurous buyer/collector can now go from town to town from city to city across the United States in search of malls and shops. A big help for the traveler, aside from the many trade publications (see Chapter 2), are the antiques shop guides in various regions of the country. A great grouping of these is contained in *Maloney's Antiques and Collectibles Resource Directory.* However, no publication or directory can contain them all. For one thing, they can pop up overnight, and in some towns the growth of these malls and shops stocked with "needful" things of the past are clearly a wave of the future. So how many antiques shops and malls does the eager paper collector have to choose from in this decade? The national newsletter *Inside Antiques* published information from a New York research firm in November of 1991 indicating that the number of antiques shop-malls had tripled in just eight years to 60,000 nationwide.

Such information, also published in the highly regarded *Collector News,* turned a few heads in the antiques crowd. Some people just could not believe so many shops were tucked away across the country. And yet, it pretty well followed the findings of other independent researchers, such as the editor of one state trade publication who estimated there were 1,500 such malls and shops in that particular state. Having researched this estimate, the editor was in considerable disagreement with a newspaper-chain group which, in preparing a guide on antiques shops, said there were around 700 shops and such in the state. Eventually, it was learned that the newspaper group had used staff members to telephone librarians in communities throughout the state. They, in turn, were asked to check the *Yellow Pages* and count the number of antiques shop listings. A good many malls and shops do not necessarily advertise in the *Yellow Pages,* which are generally directed at local residents. Most shops opt for shop guides, regional trade publications, national

publications, and out-of-town newspapers. Others use billboards, radio and television, and direct mail. The potential paper collectibles buyer, therefore, has many places to look when venturing out on the road.

SHOPPING BY MAIL

Unlike collectors of antique furniture, for example, people who collect paper items can be very well served by mail order. Potential buyers consult a published catalog, which includes a cutoff date by which bids must be received. Those interested submit bids by mail, telephone, or fax anytime before the printed deadline and are notified if theirs was the winning bid.

A good example of the appeal of mail-order paper collectibles—and the success of it, too—is Hake's Americana & Collectibles (PO Box 1444, York, PA 17405). Hake's, which has been in operation since 1967, handles 15,000 items each year through both mail auctions and in-person sales. A typical catalog ($7.50 each or $30 for five annually) contains over 3,000 items with photographs and estimated values. The topics range from political-presidential to Disney and cowboy heroes. Hake's also continues to experiment with specialized mail-order auctions, such as those featuring World War II, Disneyana, and baby-boomer comic characters.

Clearly, not everything sold here is paper, but a great deal of it is, and the depth of what is available is amazing—from an 1860s Abraham Lincoln carte de visite and an 1870s Grant presidential campaign advertising card to a store sign portraying Tom Mix and a *Leave It to Beaver* coloring book.

Cohasco, Inc. [Postal 821, Yonkers, NY 10702, (914) 476-8500] specializes in historical documents. Their twice-yearly 80-page catalogs listing 600 or more items are good examples of the quality and volume in the marketplace of these types of collectibles. Most items require bids by mail, although some may be purchased outright, and the lots are shipped to the successful bidders.

COME ALL YOU TRUE BORN DEMOCRATS,
YOU HARDY HEARTS OF OAK,
WHO KNOW A THING WHEN IT IS GOOD
AND BLACWELL'S DURHAM SMOKE.
GAZE ON THIS FACE AND YOU WILL SEE
YOUR PRESIDENTIAL NOMINEE.
THE SAGE AND STATESMAN S.J.T.

AND ALL YOU GOOD REPUBLICANS
WILL SURELY BE ENCHANTED,
WHEN YOU BEHOLD THE VISAGE HERE,
AND TAKE THE FACT FOR GRANTED
THAT HE WILL WIN, IF HE WILL BE
YOUR PRESIDENTIAL NOMINEE,
THE SOLDIER HERO U.S. G.
BUT THOUGH YOU DIFFER IN YOUR VIEWS
POLITICAL, WE HOPE
YOU COINCIDE WHEN WE REMARK,
THE CHOICEST BRAND TO SMOKE
IS BLACKWELL'S GENUINE DURHAM, THAT
SUITS EVERY TASTE NO MATTER WHAT,
REPUBLICAN OR DEMOCRAT.

*General Grant on tobacco advertising card, ca.
1872–1876. Photo courtesy of Hake's Americana
& Collectibles.*

*Abraham Lincoln and son carte de visite, 1860s.
Photo courtesy of Hake's Americana & Collectibles.*

Looking through a Cohasco catalog, a collector can expect to see things like 19th-century letters from the Queens County Agricultural Society, a letter from the wife of noted jurist Charles Evans Hughes, a fine photo print of William Jennings Bryan, or an 1898 pastel-colored map of Pennsylvania. Specialized subjects include Americana, anti-Semitism, authors, aviation, black history, Civil War, books, broadsides, famous people, maps, movies, music, newspapers, political, presidential, sports, and both World War I and World War II.

Another typically fine source of early advertising, auto literature, patriotic posters, entertainment memorabilia, and other paper collectibles is the Miscellaneous Man [PO Box 1000, New Freedom, PA 17349, (717) 235-4766]. A fully illustrated catalog, which costs about $7.50, lists approximately 1,000 items which are sold directly to the buyer and are not subject to mail bid. "We can't tell you what we have unless you tell us what you want," declares owner George Theofiles in his catalog. "Virtually all of our catalogs are the tip of the iceberg—we can list only a part of our vast inventory. Items come and go every day. If you have a special want, don't hesitate to tell us."

This type of business is both a key to success and a keyhole to the future. Buyers will find specialists like Theofiles able to pin down very selective types of paper collectibles or be able to acquire almost anything in a very short time. Theofiles was undoubtedly ahead of his time when a national magazine noted a few years ago, "After years of scouring basements and attics, rummaging through printing plants, and pleading with subject-theme

Leave It to Beaver *coloring book, 1958, Saalfield Publishing Co. Photo courtesy of Hake's Americana & Collectibles.*

collectors, Theofiles knows how to conjure up posters from Rio de Janerio to the Black Forest, and how to pin down their value in a shifting sea of fashion." Items offered by Miscellaneous Man can range from a 1957 Chrysler showroom catalog and a 1940 Chesterfield cigarette ad featuring baseball player Stan Musial to a 1969 group of anti-Vietnam student-strike posters from Harvard and large quantities of early 20th-century material.

Here are some examples of other mail-order operations:

History-Makers, 4040 East 82nd St., Indianapolis, IN 46250, (800) 424-9259. Their illustrated catalogs ($35 annually) feature mostly autographs of famous people, but there are also newspapers, posters, and other items on a direct-purchase basis.

Historic Originals, 4424 Trescott Dr., Orlando, FL 32817-3158, (407) 677-7660. Their annual catalog ($3) lists labels,

documents, and country store paper collectibles, most at nominal direct-purchase prices.

Even more specialized paper collectibles markets would include:

Lenore's *TV Guides,* PO Box 246, Three Bridges, NJ 08887, (908) 788-0532. A nifty catalog ($2) lists every *TV Guide,* from the first to those issued in the 1990s. All direct purchase by mail.

David Newell-Shaker literature, 39 Steady Lane, Ashfield, MA 01330. Catalog, 80 pages, lists about 300 items including pamphlets, seed bags, billheads, and labels relating to the religious sect.

Another alternative for the too-busy-to-travel stay-at-home are the home-shopping TV networks. Most of the paper they handle is of fairly recent manufacture, such as "modern" comic books, posters, trading (non-sports) cards, programs, and various books. Watching these programs, in my opinion, is fascinating television. However, in every example I was personally able to check through other sources, i.e., from leading specialized dealers to Walmart, I found the "shopping" price to be excessive. This leads me to believe that most of the home-shopping-network buyers are inexperienced people who are not even remotely familiar with other purchasing avenues for this type of merchandise. At the same time, I would be wary of anyone's glib claims that shopping-network items will surely rise in value. Where will the demand be and how long will it be there? (Oops, there goes the home-shopping network sales of this book.)

AUCTIONS

The prospective buyer/collector can step into the big leagues by dealing with the major auctions houses around the country. Increasingly, for example, Skinner, Inc. is handling paper collectibles. Skinner's [63 Park Plaza, Boston, MA 02116, (617) 350-5400] has long been one of the nation's leading auction galleries. The curious can expect to find special sales on books and manuscripts which offer a 1776 broadside from the Massachusetts House of Representatives or an 1861 appointment signed by Abraham Lincoln. The selection can also range from a typed document signed by *To Kill A Mockingbird* author Harper Lee to a group of land deeds and probate documents from the Middle Atlantic states of Virginia, Maryland, North Carolina, and South Carolina.

Besides single items, Skinner's offers more and more group lots, such as 35 items on Indians and cowboys dating from 1844 to 1926. A lot, which includes documents relating to Indian affairs from the Smithsonian Institution bureau of American Ethnology, might have a relatively modest pre-sale estimate of $200 to $300. But since this is an auction market, prices could be higher or lower (usually no lower than half the pre-sale estimate).

The best bet with Skinner's is a $15 subscription to their bimonthly bulletin which gives dates of upcoming auctions and general descriptions and illustrations of items being offered. The subscription also includes an annual newsletter with reviews of auctions. Their catalogs, meanwhile, are detailed and well illustrated, but very few are devoted exclusively to paper collectibles.

At the top of the paper collectibles marketplace is Swann Galleries in New York City. Every year Swann [104 East 25th St., New York, NY 10010, (212) 979-1017] conducts more than 30 auctions, which bring worldwide attention to posters, prints, books, autographs, maps, photographs, and even magic-related collectibles. They also do at least one auction per year of pure ephemera, featuring calling cards, Civil War paper, magazines, newspapers, match covers, rewards of merit, trade cards, and dozens of other paper subjects. At the ephemera auctions, the collector might run into a broadside for a 1872 lecture by Kit Carson, an autograph by Babe Ruth, an early edition of Beckett's *Monthly Baseball Price Guide,* or a group of souvenir letterheads from the Columbian Exposition.

This varied and efficient firm was founded in 1941 and now maintains separate departments for such areas as works of art on paper, photographs and photographic literature, and autographs and manuscripts. Their manuscripts and books, incidentally, like other aspects of their merchandise, range from Shakespeare to Stephen King.

George Lowery the president of Swann Galleries is sometimes called the Six-Million-Dollar Man. He took over operation of the company at the retirement of founder Benjamin Swann in 1969 and guided it through a series of sales which topped $6 million dollars annually by 1991. Perhaps the most exciting areas of growth have been in the sales of photographs and autographs. Today, for example, Swann's is one of the largest sources for Civil War materials, conveniently touching on both areas.

Lowery predicted that autographs will generally do well throughout the decade noting that "autographs continue to get a lot of public attention." Meanwhile, "Movies we know are going well and so are the stars associated with them. At this time people feel they are buying blue-chip investment items." According to Lowry, the book business remains good even while economic tides come and go. "People who collect books are fairly conservative and fairly established," confides Lowry. "It is my theory that they will continue to indulge themselves."

What is changing in the paper collectibles marketplace, in Lowry's view, are the buyers. "More and more private people are getting involved in buying at auction. This is especially true with photographs," he notes, "but it extends to other areas as well." What once may have just been a group of dealers has evolved, at least at the major auction galleries dealing with paper collectibles, into a worldwide audience of collectors, investors, and others. Some 60 to 70 percent of Swann's swelling business is from mail-order customers.

Their auctions are typically advertised in popular, specialized, and trade publications.

About a month before each sale auction catalogs with details and pre-sale estimates for each item are available. People can, of course, personally attend each auction, but the majority do not. They make use of the mail, telephone or fax. Potential buyers can call the expert in charge to discuss an aspect of the sale or, for a small fee, can order photographs of particular items of interest. Serious customers can make advanced arrangements to bid by telephone during the sale, but this is generally reserved for high-rollers who expect to bid at least in the range of the highest estimate. If using the telephone system, sources at Swann warn, "Be prepared to act decisively, because the pace is brisk. We average 100 to 150 lots per hour." Interested collector/buyers can also request a complimentary subscription to Swann's newsletter, *The Trumpet,* which is distributed quarterly.

Collectors' Newsletters

One reason the marketplace is exploding is the growing diversity of collectors. Someone in Akron, Ohio, may collect Goodyear paper memorabilia because a long line of family members worked there or just for the heck of it. Whatever the reason, an individual collector thus becomes a specific buyer in a specific field. The next thing you know, there is a group of Goodyear collectors and, perhaps, eventually a full-fledged collectible area complete with listings in various price books. Ultimately, the interest could lead to a collectibles guide on Goodyear paper. And even if things don't develop that far, there is a good possibility of a publication, at least a newsletter, devoted to that category of paper collectible.

Here are some examples of specialized publications and organizations:

American Antique Graphics Society provides catalogs and corresponding videos on rare paper and labels. AAGS, 5185 Windfall Rd., Medina, OH 44256, (216) 723-3333.

Antique Label Collector, PO Box 24811, Tampa, FL 33623.

McDonald's Collectors Club newsletter, 5400 Waterbury Rd., Des Moines, IA 50312.

Past Times newsletter (antique advertising), PO Box 1121, Morton Grove, IL 60055.

Autograph Review newsletter, 305 Carlton Rd., Syracuse, NY 13207.

Baseball Autograph News, 527 Third Ave. #294, New York, NY 10016.

Cookbook Gossip newsletter, PO Box 56, St. James, MO 65559.

Illustrator Collector's News newsletter (books), PO Box 1958, Sequim, WA 98382.

International Paperback Collectors Society newsletter (collectible paperbacks), 21 Deer Lane, Wantagh, NY 11793.

Playboy Collectors Association newsletter, Rt. 1, Box 3020, Phillipsburg, MO 65722.

Naturally, many of the newsletters and groups involved in producing them are still another marketplace for the collector/buyer. "Publications for the Collector," a list of about 900 specialized resources is available for $3 from Antiques, Inc. at PO Box 22900, Beachwood, OH 44122.

The potential buyer/collector/investor also has a great many price guides to consider. *Warman's Paper,* by Norman Martinus and Harry Rinker, is far and away the best guide available on paper collectibles at this writing. However, I would recommend having several general price guides on hand, including *Schroeder's Antiques Price Guide, The Garage Sale and Flea Market Annual, and Kovels' Antiques & Collectibles Price List, Warman's Antiques and Collectibles Price Guide, 29th Edition,* and *Warman's Americana & Collectibles, 6th Edition* to name a few. Most users find they have to consult numerous related categories to find a specific price for an unusual paper item. A pack of

Half and Half cigarettes from the 1960s might not be under paper, packs, or even tobacco, but simply cigarette collectibles.

It is my opinion that older, used, and often discarded price guides can be most helpful for research. They enable the collector to pinpoint price ranges on assorted paper for a particular year and provide current comparisons. Usually these "outdated" price guides are available at very modest cost.

SPECIALTY SHOWS

A word about shows. There are a rapidly growing number of shows specializing in paper collectibles throughout the United States. Some offer only one particular type of item and others combine books, comics, trading cards, or other related categories. Moreover, not only is the nature of major shows expanding and changing, but the times and locations of forthcoming events are somewhat elusive to pinpoint.

A good resource to consult for the latest schedules is the previously mentioned *Paper Collectors' Marketplace* [PO Box 128, Scandinavia, WI 54977-0128, (715) 467-2379]. Typically, each monthly issue lists 10 to 12 major national and regional shows with specific dates and locations. The lists are updated and corrected every month and are about as accurate as possible within the time frame. Still, it is a very good idea to call ahead to determine the status of any show before traveling a long distance. Things do change, as do marketplaces.

CHAPTER FIVE

The State of Paper Collectibles

One of the soundest rules I try to remember when making forecasts in the field of economics is that whatever is to happen is happening already.
—*Sylvia Porter*

• •

There was a time when only certain people collected antiques and, even then, many unwritten rules applied. When the collectibles crowd came along with their baseball cards, Ginny dolls, and Little Golden Books things changed. Now they are changing again. Paper collectibles can be anything from Lincoln memorabilia to place mats from McDonald's. There are no real rules on what to collect or how to enjoy it. The old dealer's axiom was never more true: Anything you possess has a collector out there somewhere looking for it.

With the coming of the age of diversity in paper collectibles also comes the generation of specialization. If, as statistics show, there are 50,000 members of the Official Star Trek Club, 15,000 members of the Andy Griffith Rerun Watchers Club, and 200 people who

Cheyenne *Little Golden Book, 1958. Photo courtesy of Hake's Americana & Collectibles.*

Wyatt Earp record, 45 rpm, Peter Pan label, 1958. Photo courtesy of Hake's Americana & Collectibles.

Roy Rogers with Trigger, wire service photo, 1954.

collect police cars, there are bound to be a dozen people out there who collect the printed tags of leading clothing designers. Moreover, besides diversity and specialization, nearly every category of paper collectibles has secondary levels. If for example, collectors of Roy Rogers and Gene Autry memorabilia can no longer find or afford signed photographs, they will move to advertisements, wire-service photographs, or anything else which connects to the cowboy movie genre.

CURRENT COLLECTING TRENDS

Two world-class experts on the development of antiques and collecting in the 20th century are Ralph and Terry Kovel. In the past 40 years, they have produced more than 60 books on various aspects of it. "It's interesting that when we started collecting in our 20s, we bought things 200, 150, or 100 years old, because that was what was considered good enough to buy" they noted in an interview with *American Country Collectibles* magazine in 1993. Now for collectors, "50 years back is considered a long way, and much further back than 1900 they just plain don't like—they don't want any part of it, it's not part of their environment. Now they're buying McDonald's throwaways."

The Kovels and a few others have for some time realized that most new treasures will be gathered from the 1950s, 1960s, and 1970s. "The 40-year-old with money who watched all those television shows like *Leave It to Beaver* are making all that stuff very collectible. To them it represents Grandma." "So things are changing," the two told writer

Paul Slimak, "and you never know what people will buy next. For a number of years we used to do an April Fool's article about strange collectibles, but we can't do it anymore because no one would think it's a joke."

Another change underway for some time has been from the traditional to the untried. People want to collect things which are not over regulated and graded or in endless supply. Todd Axelrod, chief executive officer of Gallery of History, a firm that buys and sells documents signed by the likes of Daniel Boone, Winston Churchill, Walt Disney, Babe Ruth, Lou Gehrig, and Harry Houdini, has said that many stamp and coin collectors have jumped ship to signed documents.

Axelrod told *USA Today* in 1993 that the number of collectors of historical documents had risen from only 30,000 in 1989 to 80,000 four years later. In three years, according to Axelrod, total revenues for historical documents in this country—once in the $8 to $10 million annual range—have doubled. He added that sales were divided primarily between auctions and private transactions.

Nor is the new wave of paper collectibles totally comparable to another field or a long-ago generation. They say that 19th-century author Mark Twain often received photographs from people who had convinced themselves that they looked like him. Finally, Twain's workplace was overrun with pictures of people who thought they could almost pass for his twin. At last the famed author prepared a form letter reply to all the hopefuls. It read like this:

My dear Sir:

I thank you very much for your letter and your photograph. In my opinion you are more like me than any other of my numerous doubles. I may even say that you resemble me more closely than I do myself. In fact, I intend to use your picture to shave by.

Yours thankfully, S. Clemens.

The state of paper collectibles is much like that. It may look similar to something else, but as it emerges, it will have an image entirely different from all others.

FUTURE PAPER COLLECTIBLES

As the 1990s began, a national poll was conducted on just where in time people would rather be living if they had a choice. The results showed more than 80 percent would prefer to have lived sometime in the past. It is ironic that as the more things change, the more people wish they could be living in a time unaffected by it all.

Nearly 8,000 Americans move each day from the country to the city, and another 5,000 move from the city to the country. The vast majority of them leave behind boxes of discarded, abandoned, or just plain forgotten belongings and memories.

There are 6,500 couples married each day in this country, and more than 600,000 people celebrate birthdays, including 11,000 who turn 40 and 6,000 who turn 65. We collectively acknowledge these occasions with nine million greeting cards each day. On Valentine's Day the average person receives 4 cards, and for Christmas the average is 12 per person. Someday we'll wished we had saved them all. And if we didn't, we may find ourselves searching out the shops and flea markets for cards exactly like them.

At a slightly more mundane level, mailboxes and post office boxes in the United States are filled with 5,000 tons of advertising mail each day, including 20 million catalogs. Some day some of the 20 different catalogs published each day will be collectible. The climate, then, offers more choices of present-day paper collectibles than ever before in history.

COMPETITION AMONG COLLECTORS

To those who choose to collect on a more sophisticated level than 20th-century greeting cards or catalogs, the competition in the future will be significant. Gallery of History's CEO Axelrod tells of purchasing a George

Washington letter for $4,700 and later selling it for $110,000. He also reportedly bought a real-estate contract signed by Marilyn Monroe for her Brentwood, California, home for $500 and later sold it for $15,000. (That makes you sort of want to search your company's old business files for any contracts signed by important people.)

Movie star Debbie Reynolds collects paper movie memorabilia, among other things, and has her own museum in Las Vegas. "I went to auctions of Hollywood memorabilia and bought everything," she once told TV host Larry King on CNN, "I loved it all." The wife of movie idol Gregory Peck once told an interviewer of his "burning interest, love, affection, and fascination" for Lincoln and Lincoln memorabilia, as well as material relating to the Civil War. In the summer of 1991, at a leading New York City auction gallery, Wayne Newton spent $13,200 for a letter handwritten by Elvis Presley, comedian Eddie Murphy paid $30,000 for Jimi Hendrix rock memorabilia, and an Italian concert promoter put in a top bid of $35,000 for Hendrix's handwritten lyrics to "Room Full of Mirrors."

President Bill Clinton may not himself be into paper collectibles but he is aware of their potential. The president told a summer jobs conference in 1993 that when he was 13 years old, around 1959 or early 1960, he botched his first business deal, although he didn't know it until later. Clinton explained how he set up a comic book stand and "made more money than I ever had in my life" selling off two trunks of comic books. "If I'd saved those trunks, they'd be worth $100,000 today," he quipped.

Movie actor Maximilian Schell, a distinguished collector of many things including musical material and books, once told *Architectural Digest,* "If you know, especially in collecting, a little bit of what's good and what's bad, it means power. If you know these things early enough, you can get things that later on represent a certain power." Certainly, the rich and famous, from rock stars to

stock market kingpins, seek the "power" of acquiring some highly desirable paper collectibles, just as do others from different stations in life.

In the future the competition will be heavier at the major auction galleries as they gradually increase their activity in paper collectibles. Likewise other more traveled routes will become busier as the serious collector encounters others with the same mind. The hunt for the traditional, from trading cards to Little Golden Books and postcards to sports magazines, will greatly depend on what can be found along the byways of grass-roots America, where the high rollers do not have the time or inclination to look. Hunts for garage sales in the hinterlands, for example, will look better and better in the search for unmined paper collectible treasures.

Emerging areas with little previous fanfare will attract more attention and more collectors. These include space exploration memorabilia, John F. Kennedy mementos, children's coloring books, sports magazines,

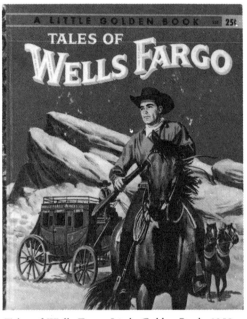

Tales of Wells Fargo *Little Golden Book, 1958. Photo courtesy of Hake's Americana & Collectibles.*

Wizard of Oz *sound track record album, MGM label, 1950s. Photo courtesy of Hake's Americana & Collectibles.*

Official media kit, Kennedy family photo, 1960.

Hee Haw *coloring book, Saalfield Publishing Co., 1970. Photo courtesy of Hake's Americana & Collectibles.*

wire-service photographs, rock-and-roll souvenirs, paper dolls, the counterculture and war-protest posters and leaflets, postcards with contemporary advertising, art calendars of the 1980s, Christmas catalogs, trading-card display boxes, greeting cards, record albums, adult paperbacks, and fast-food memorabilia.

Another avenue which will be a departure from the traditional, concerns discovering paper collectibles which have a potential future but not much of a past. In other words, a category which has not yet been the subject of several articles or a single price guide. Possible topics include the Vietnam War, baseball card price guide publications, catalogs of specialized topics, greeting cards (especially Hallmark), business cards, driver's licenses, press credentials, travel brochures, pioneering travel facilities signs of the 1970s from the Department of Transportation, nuclear-attack advisory material of all types, 1940s and 1950s bus schedules, and early cigarette packages or related material.

Sometimes it will be a matter of simply updating an already established paper collectibles area. For example, fancy lace valentines from the turn of the century have long been popular, but the much more colorful comic

Mt. Rainier National Park, Tacoma, Washington, travel brochure, 1949.

Fallout shelter sign, ca. 1960. Photo courtesy of The Strong Museum, Rochester, New York.

Liberty magazine, boxing cover, June 13, 1936.

valentines of the 1940s, 1950s, and 1960s are still waiting to be discovered.

COLLECTING AS AN INVESTMENT

For many the thrill of the paper chase is enough. Gleaning one Helen Clapsaddle holiday card out of a handful of old postcards, turning over a box of old sports programs,

Tropic Lightning News, *Vietnam era newspaper,*
March 1968.

finding a stack of 1960s TV-show coloring
books, or capturing a photograph of some of
the legends of the Old West is what it is all
about. But experiences like that lead to collections and collections lead to—whether intended or not—accumulated value. From this
decade on, serious collectors will clearly realize that their collection represents an investment of both time and money, no matter how
diverse the amount.

In the future, the investment aspect of
acquiring paper collectibles will be impossible to ignore, even if the purist would have it
differently. There are some points to consider
in the years ahead, therefore, to enhance the
investment aspect of collecting.

1. Buy at a good price. Pay no more than
going market value unless absolutely necessary. Of course, if you can purchase an item at
a fraction of the market value, you have already made a solid profit from the investment. As one kindly dealer likes to remind
me, you make your money when you buy the
paper not when you sell it.

2. Acquire top quality. Remember good
is always good, and faded and raggedy will
always remain that way too.

3. Collect what pleases you and do not be
rushed into parting with it. If you are going to
need cash, invest in a savings account and not
paper collectibles. It won't look as good in a
frame, but you will have immediate access to
your money. Rushing out to unload your 1939
Silver Streak Pontiac showroom booklet, the
John Wayne movie poster, and the Mickey

Mantle cover of *Life Magazine* in order to
make your car payment could be very foolish.
The wise investor will purchase paper which
is aesthetically enriching, display it in his
home, decorate with it, and share it with
others. Enjoying the items on a regular basis
makes long-term investing relatively easy to
deal with. Remember, for example, it may
take months to sell prized paper material.
This is especially true if dealing with mail-
order auctions or auctions at leading galleries.
It has been my experience that those who are
best suited for investing are those paper collectors who have the greatest interest in the
collection and are willing to spend a considerable amount of time studying the market,
waiting, and enjoying. To those people, financial gain is of secondary importance to actually having the material on hand.

4. Stay tuned and in touch. Read the
trade magazines and newspapers, the auction
catalogs, the dealers' lists, new price guides,
and everything else you can find. All these
things inform you and make you a wiser
collector. And, like it or not, they often have a
direct effect on the marketplace.

5. Make yours a true collection and not
just an accumulation. If it is well organized
and well cared for, it will have more meaning
while you own it and far more value when and
if you sell it. Keep good records of your paper
items, noting when and where the material
was acquired and for what cost, if any. (Also
bear in mind that much of the ultimate profits
from paper could be subject to federal tax
and proper records may be vital.) The ownership history or provenance of paper items can
be very important to the future of your collection. Was that colonial newspaper John
Adams' own personal copy with his name on
it? Did that collection of movie-star arcade
cards come directly from the Joan Crawford
estate? Was grandfather a printer at the plant
and did he save a copy when the first *Playboy*
rolled off the press?

Generally speaking, in the state of the
market ahead, most all paper collectibles will
appreciate in value over the years. In some
cases the values will fluctuate from time to

time but, ultimately, most will reflect at least some gains. (If you want to test this theory, dig out some old price guides—ten years old or older—and compare the price listings with the current value of similar paper collectibles. It's almost impossible to find an item that has not increased in value.)

Many serious dealer/collectors build a collection of certain paper collectibles, enjoy them for a time, and then sell for a profit, only to start reinvesting in still another paper collection. It enables a person of relatively modest means to own a great number of fine paper collectibles over a lifetime and make a bit of a profit. With some exceptions, prices for interesting paper are still relatively low compared to many other collectibles, plus there is still the chance of finding real treasures at garage sales or even some flea markets. Meanwhile, interest is growing not only with individuals and investors, but also with organizations, corporations, universities, and associations, many of which are buying up paper to add to their own permanent archives. And once material is acquired by a university library, for example, it is rarely put back into the marketplace.

One final note for the investor: Paper collectibles which are limited in supply now were not necessarily in scarce production at their inception. During the 1940s and 1950s, for instance, some comic books were produced in the hundreds of thousands or even millions, but hardly anyone saved them. They were read and re-read, folded, rolled, and finally tossed away—as they were intended to be. Today, of course, those copies that survived in very good condition are nearly priceless. So the ultimate supply, not simply the original quantities produced, becomes a major factor in collecting paper material.

As bright as the future of paper collectibles may be, there is also a downside. The basics of living are taking such a large share of American household incomes that the antiques and collectibles industry may take up residence in the bargain basement.

In 1973, America's best-selling car, a Chevrolet, cost $3,771 or about 39 percent of the median household income. Nearly 20 years later, the best-selling car, this time a Ford, cost $15,280 or 49 percent of the median household income. During the early 1970s, the price of a home was 2.8 times the median household income. During the early 1990s, the cost of a home rose to 3.3 times the household income.

Not so long ago, the price of the daily newspaper was not very important. If things were in a slump, the publisher just raised the price of the newspaper and hardly anyone noticed. It was a very simplistic approach to a complex problem, and one which had unprecedented results in the 1990s. One leading daily newspaper in Florida raised the price of the paper five times in three years during the 1990s. Circulation dropped by the thousands—one out of every ten subscribers quit rather than paying a few cents more for a paper.

In the final analysis, everyone is looking for a better deal and is willing to move in different directions to find it. Like the retail market before it, the paper collectibles market will have bargain basements built in because the times and the buyers demand it.

CHAPTER SIX

Collecting Tips and Strategies

*"You don't need to be helped any longer. You've always had
the power to go back to Kansas."*
—The Good Witch to Dorothy
Wizard of Oz

• •

DO YOUR HOMEWORK

Given the right information, or at least knowing the right place to look for it, you can go about the business of acquiring paper collectibles with some confidence. You sort of put the expert shoes on before leaving home.

One thing you should do is avidly read the classified advertisements of the various collector publications, especially the "wanted" ads in trade newspapers and magazines around the country. Pretty soon, you'll know what collectors are readily willing to pay, you'll know how they go beyond the routine in obtaining it, and you'll know what the competition is for the paper memorabilia that you want. In short, you will acquire a very different view of the marketplace. You will likely find there is already demand for dental, automotive, and computer material from the 1940s to the 1970s, for gas station paper items of various eras, advertising labels, military manuals, and paper material which focuses on specific states or regions of the country.

Besides the periodicals, there are books (i.e., *Wanted To Buy, Where To Sell It, I'll Buy That, Kovels' Guide to Selling Your Antiques & Collectibles, Who's Who in Collecting and Antiques,* and others) which provide even greater access to this material. This kind of don't-leave-home-without-it homework pays off in many ways, including demonstrating how really diverse paper collectibles can

be and that most anything of paper in good condition can have a potential collector.

Another expert shoe to wear are lists. When my wife and I finally became business partners, we took the mundane grocery list and made it a state-of-the-art communications network for the entire operation. In short, we made a list of everything. Little

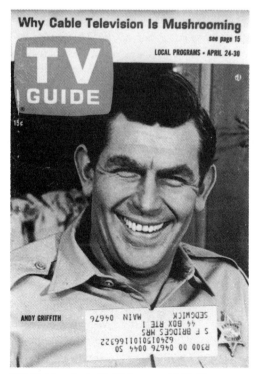

TV Guide, *Andy Griffith cover, 1965. Photo courtesy of Hake's Americana & Collectibles.*

Walt Disney's Lady and the Tramp Album *comic book, Dell, 1955. Photo courtesy of Hake's Americana & Collectibles.*

Walt Disney's Magazine, *1957. Photo courtesy of Hake's Americana & Collectibles.*

Golden Books, comic books, *TV Guides,* advertising cards, Disneyana, magazines, calendars, trading cards, View-Master albums, photographs—whatever the collection, it pays to take a list of needs and wants, as well as inventory, when you go on the road.

Of course, in this age of digital technology, the specifics of your paper collection wants need not be scribbled on the back of the envelope that the utility bill came in. Computer technology allows you to pack all that data in your pocket, so do it.

Visiting antiques shops and malls, flea markets, museums, and occasional auctions is not only great fun but a seminar on the antique and collectible things of paper as well. There is no better single way to absorb the current marketplace and become knowledgeable in the field then to visit half a dozen antiques malls over a weekend. A potential investor or collector can also head to the public library. Often price guides from previous years are available for item-by-item com-

parisons. Then too, consult the library's selection of books on investing. Check the index of some of the most interesting ones, approximately 10 to 20 percent offer advice of various degrees on investing in collectibles.

A few years ago the Manhattan hotel Novotel New York did a survey of their guests and found that 252 people had locked themselves out of their rooms that year, more than two-thirds of them women. Moreover 74 guests, again about two-thirds women, had locked themselves out of their room while stark naked.

So the lesson here is don't leave without your homework, your lists, and your clothing.

FINE POINTS TO PONDER
Seeking Out Paper Collectibles

There is a story about a fabled mountain 100 miles high and 100 miles wide. Every 100 years, a small bird flies by and stops to sharpen his tiny beak. When that mountain is

Boys' Life *magazine, Mickey Mantle cover, August 1959. Photo courtesy of Hake's Americana & Collectibles.*

Jayne Mansfield *calendar for 1961. Photo courtesy of Hake's Americana & Collectibles.*

worn away, so the story goes, one day of eternity will have passed. A peck of that beak, as far as the paper collectibles marketplace is concerned, is the *Paper Collectors Monthly* (details in chapter four), which averages 97 pages and includes 220 display ads and more than 1,200 classified ads in a typical issue. As good and complete as this publication is, it offers only a clue to the potential of paper collectibles.

There are little old ladies with boxes in their attics and rarefied merchants with personalized videos, all representing possible sources for collectible material. Some collectors would never pass up the opportunity to search out attics and old garages even if it involves hours of consuming dust while armed with nothing more than a flashlight and a notebook. Others prefer the specialized video route where, for example, an organization like the American Antique Graphics Society supplies a televised look at the inventory of their next auction in the comfort of your own home. The group can provide the collec-

tor with everything from a 13th-century copy of the Ten Commandments on an illuminated Bible leaf (estimated value $650 to $750) to a book of 107 sample turn-of-the-century cigar bands from American Lithograph (estimated value $175 to $225).

The oldest and most prestigious of paper collectibles dealers would be the two icons of the auction gallery world, Christie's International and Sotheby's. Both originated in the 1700s, both are distinguished for their meticulous attention to detail, and together they control the lion's share of the art and antiques industry. As a journalist long in the field of antiques and collectibles, I find the staffs of slightly smaller auction houses such as Skinner's or Swann's much more receptive and somewhat more accommodating, but the stature of Christie's and Sotheby's is undeniable.

"This isn't quite a monopoly, but a global duopoly is almost as good," wrote Peter Lynch in a leading financial magazine in 1994. Lynch, vice-chairman of Fidelity Management and Research and former manager of the record-setting Magellan Fund, added, "You and I and $500 million could hire some scientists and invent a new computer chip, but we couldn't mount a serious threat against Christie's and Sotheby's."

The auction market has grown annually in recent years at the rate of 15 percent worldwide, mainly to the credit of these two giants. That growth was clearly not inhibited by Sotheby's gradual addition of categories such as comic books, baseball cards, paper rock-and-roll memorabilia, and original sketches for Disney animated cartoons. Like paper collectibles, the future of the auction gallery elite remains bright and sunny.

"Every decade seems to produce a different group of rich buyers who want to acquire the high-priced treasures of formerly rich sellers who need the cash (the Arabs in the 1970s, the Japanese in the 1980s)" concludes Lynch. "As long as there's death, divorce, changes of address, and reversals of fortune, we'll see no end to the procession of goods out of one drawing room and into another. Sotheby's will be there to collect the commission both ways." And so will be a lot of other progressive auction houses.

• •

THERE IS SOMETHING I LIKE TO APPLY TO THE paper collectibles field that is known as the Halloween rule. Not withstanding that Halloween was always my favorite holiday, in truth it was once a relatively obscure observance, which is now second only to Christmas in popularity. (Did people living in small American towns ever dream that about half the houses and yards would some day be annually decorated not just for Christmas but Halloween as well?)

Consider the fact that much of the paper surrounding the pumpkin holiday, like candy bags used for trick or treat, Halloween party invitations, event posters, and the like, were used and then discarded. So combine a custom or event that gradually soars in popularity with the inevitable loss of paper memorabilia which surrounded it, and you have a highly collectible result—the Halloween rule.

• •

Recognizing Future Collectibles

One of the many opportunities in the paper collectibles field, as I see it, is being alert enough and foresighted enough to pick up attractive and colorful items before they become objects of widespread desire. Consider the video movie and the box it came in. For years, nearly a generation, these colorful boxes held the most appealing and intriguing films in the world. Experts now predict that because of the onset of the so-called information highway, videos are doomed.

Who would trundle down to the video store some dark night, the argument goes, when one could electronically select from thousands of shows right at home? In the

Paper bag for Halloween treats, orange and black.

future, videos could become as obsolete as long-playing record albums. So what becomes, then, of the wonderfully illustrated video boxes that are virtually small movie posters of the great and not-so-great films? They go out of use, are discarded in vast numbers, and eventually may reach lofty collectible status as the paper memorabilia of movies past. And also remember, the video stores today are great sources for movie posters and cardboard figures of current movie heroes.

Then there is television itself. According to the U.S. Department of Commerce, more American households have TV sets—about 98 percent—than indoor plumbing. In 1960 people watched about 5 hours of TV per day; 30 years later the average daily viewing time is slightly over 7 hours. The average American preschool child watches more than 27 hours of TV per week, that's about 4 hours per day.

In 1993, Associated Press carried a story nationally about a businessman and former rock-radio producer in Philadelphia who felt rock-and-roll memorabilia would eventually be as hot as sports collectibles were in the 1980s and early 1990s. "If someone doesn't preserve it, the only way you're ever going to find it is if you go to a used record store," explained the dealer, adding that buying record albums just for the cover art is already a luxury. Not surprisingly, one of the fastest-growing segments of business at Sotheby's and at Christie's in the 1990s is the auctioning of rock memorabilia. The answer for the Philadelphia dealer was to market lithographs of 18 major rock album covers dating from 1965 to 1981. These images sold splendidly at $300 to $400 each. Customers figured that was the only way to obtain the likes of Roger Dean on "Relayer," Bob Dylan's "Self-Portrait," the Eagles' "Hotel California," Cream's "Disraeli Gears," or Santana's "Abraxas."

Consider, too, just how much things like videos and rock music affect the lives of so many people, particularly younger Americans. According to the Video Software Dealers Association, there were 200 million videocassette rentals in 1982; in 1992 the number

of rentals had grown to approximately 3.6 billion. During the same 10-year period, according to the Recording Industry Association of America, the number of music-unit sales (everything from compact discs to music videos) increased more than 50 percent, to an annual total of over 900 million.

Finally, the *Journal of the American Medical Association* published a study in 1989 showing that the average teenager listens to 10,500 hours of rock music while a student in the 7th to 12th grade. According to Elizabeth Brown and William Hendee, who conducted the study "Adolescents and Their Music," that figure is just slightly less than the entire number of hours spent in the classroom from kindergarten through high school.

So what will be the hot paper collectibles when this group reaches adulthood and starts wanting the "toys" of their childhood?

Investing in Paper Collectibles

Those seriously thinking about paper collectibles as investments should consider a small story about baseballs. Baseballs signed by Ted Williams, Joe DiMaggio, and Mickey Mantle might seem like a sure thing in terms of increasing value. But it wasn't so in 1993 when a major hobby publication (*Tuff Stuff*) reported such autographed items had dropped nearly 30 percent in value. The reason was simply supply-and-demand economics. The baseball greats were signing balls at a rate greater than the number of collectors wishing to purchase them. It is no secret that some sports figures, and even a few comic book artists, are being well paid to secure themselves in a room and sign their name for hours at a time. Won't the supply eventually begin to exceed at least the serious high-dollar demand? As the beloved Luther, on TV's delightful comedy show *Coach* would say, you don't have to be a "nuclear psychiatrist" to figure that one out.

In theory, the same thing could happen if, for example, the publishers of *Boys' Life* continued to produce and sell for 25¢ the August 1959 issue with Mickey Mantle on the cover. The market would be flooded, of course, and the value of such magazines would be about the same as the issue price. Unlike baseballs, the vast majority of paper collectibles—while they may be manufactured in large numbers—are produced only for a limited time and, for the most part, were not intended to endure. As the retail source ceases production and the available supply is diminished through use, the collectibility has generally appreciated.

It is wise to not only consider how limited the supply of a particular paper item might be, but also, if possible, the past performance of similar treasures. In the early 1950s, the Quaker Oats Company included in their breakfast cereal boxes a series of trading cards which depicted the adventures of Sgt. Preston of the Yukon. The mythical hero starred first in radio and later on TV. A quarter of a century later in 1985, the trading cards were listed in the *Official Price Guide to Paper Collectibles.* The entire 35-card set was valued between $2 and $5. In 1993, one of the leading periodicals on trading cards, *Card Collector's Price Guide Monthly,* listed the same cards at $140 to $180 per set. The trading card craze and the popularity of things from the 1950s had converged.

• •

THERE IS AN IMAGINARY LINE THAT I CALL THE hero curve, which begins with the ordinary artifacts of childhood. It climbs until it reaches the point at which an adult collector many years later is willing to pay significant sums to own them once again. Ultimately, however, the hero curve declines as the adult collector whose childhood was immortalized by these objects goes to that big playland in the sky.

In early 1994 the national financial magazine *Worth* reported that items relating to 1930s cowboy hero Tom Mix were at last declining in the hero curve. The magazine quoted a dealer in Breesport, New York, as saying, "These are already selling at half what they were worth when

Tom Mix movie still, 1930s. Photo courtesy of Hake's Americana & Collectibles.

people who grew up with them were alive and buying." In fact, according to the magazine, they had declined in value by nearly 40 percent during the previous year. But this is to be considered a curve and not a full circle by any means. Tom Mix, Flash Gordon, Yellow Kid, Little Orphan Annie, the Lone Ranger, or whoever once entertained yesterday's child will always maintain a certain level of value no matter what the fate of past generations. They will never return to the virtual pennies they originally sold for.

Meanwhile, the baby boomers are "scrambling to buy a second childhood," noted the same issue of *Worth.* Consequently, prices for old toys and related memorabilia had risen 25 percent during the previous year. They cited a market-research official with Yankelovich Partners who said, "Investment in the 1950s is hotter than predicted. Toys are the most emotional part of that trend."

All this would suggest that the astute collector could accumulate paper collectibles with an eye to cashing them in as they "matured" to the 40-year-old range. Put another way, this means capturing the market for 50-year-olds who were about 10 when some of these paper products first appeared. The hero curve will not work for every paper collectible, of course, but it does have significant application.

• •

Designing with Paper Collectibles

Over the years I have seen rooms decorated with small groupings of wedding certificates, marriage licenses, bridal photographs, and related material. Sometimes the items have direct ties to earlier members of the family, and sometimes they just reflect a celebration of long-traditional occasions. In any case, the decorating style depends on the happy factor.

One of the greatest joys in paper collectibles, or any other collectible for that matter, is having the objects around you as part of your environment. Ideally, this probably means framing them (with due regard for the dangers of unfiltered light) and hanging them on the wall. If your interest is the 1960s decade, for example, imagine the fun of a display which includes newspapers, calendars, sports programs, tickets, billheads, posters, and other memorabilia from that period. No matter how splendid or breathtaking the collection of paper items, it has little impact if it is not available for easy viewing.

"The prevailing reason for collecting, both in terms of number and importance, is passion," writes Candace O. Manroe in the charming book *Designing With Collectibles.* "People collect the things they love. The primary impetus for collecting, then, is emotional. Follow your heart."

Many collectors are endowed with the ability to make wise choices and investments in paper, surround themselves with the artifacts, and enjoy that arrangement until there is a tidy profit to be made. That, clearly, is the best of both worlds.

Part II

Buyer's
Guide

· · · · · · · · · · · · · · · · · · · ·

ADVERTISING

Magazines

Famed flyer Amelia Earhart did not smoke, yet one of the tobacco industry's most famous printed advertisements of the late 1920s depicts her with a pack of Lucky Strike cigarettes. The magazine ad with Amelia's picture and facsimile signature quotes her as saying they were carried aboard the airplane *Friendship* when she crossed the Atlantic. "They were smoked continuously from Trepassey to Wales. I think nothing else helped so much to lessen the strain for all of us."

Reportedly, Miss Earhart allowed her image and signed endorsement to be used at the urging of her crew, some members of which did smoke Luckies. Given the fact that memorabilia of this flyer is far more scarce than that of her male counterpart, Charles Lindberg, plus the growing interest and appeal of female heroes in all areas, the Earhart ad is prized. One copy is in the Smithsonian Institution; others are hard to come by.

Magazine advertising involving personalities endorsing products continues to be a growing area. In this century celebrity endorsements usually came from movie stars and athletes; however, there have been other participants from astronauts to government leaders. During the 1980s a great deal of interest was generated over the many magazine advertisements that Ronald Reagan had appeared in as a movie star, long before becoming president of the United States. Collectors could find Reagan in many ads, including one showing him in Easter attire for Marlboro shirts. Mrs. Reagan, once Nancy Davis, "starred" in a magazine ad promoting Deltah stimulated pearls. Not many celebrities will become president or First Lady (or First Gentleman), but as their status changes to retirement or a new profession, or from dramatic acclaim to misfortune, the collectibility of their existing old magazine ads increases considerably.

Other areas of magazine advertisements with an established past and very potential

Amelia Earhart Lucky Strike cigarettes magazine ad, 1928.

future are those for specific companies or products, such as Campbell's Soup, Cream of Wheat, or Wheaties the "breakfast of champions." Other collectors continue to seek items related to particular topics, such as sports, aviation, soft drinks (especially Coke), motorcycles, dolls and toys, or automobiles. Beyond that, some look for overall style in printed advertisements, particularly Art Nouveau and Art Deco. In the future Art Moderne and even Postmodern styles will be recognized subcategories of this field. Most of these styles are well represented by auto advertisements, but certainly not confined to that product alone.

For generations, collecting magazine ads by specific artists has been popular. Throughout the 20th century some very fine artists lent their considerable talents to commercial magazine endeavors. Names long established include J.C. Leyendecker, Maxfield Parrish, James Montgomery Flagg, Grace Drayton, Norman Rockwell, and Jessie Wilcox Smith.

Tom Mix radio program store sign for Ralston cereal, ca. 1933. Photo courtesy of Hake's Americana & Collectibles.

In the upper ranks of collecting, there has been a trend to acquire photographs depicting scenes and products used in various actual advertisements. Those from the 1930s and 1940s, in black and white, have attracted considerable collector interest in places like Swann Galleries. The commercial works of leading photographers can bring hundreds or even thousands of dollars in many cases.

Coca-Cola

One of the great believers in print advertising over the past 100 years has been The Coca-Cola Company. Consequently, the major magazines of this country published during the first half of the century are a treasure trove of ads for this soft drink. The company's fine tradition of Christmas holiday ads featuring Santa began in the early 1930s. Prior to that time Americans generally saw the stern St. Nicholas of the European tradition, but Coke officials insisted that artist Haddon Sundblom depict Santa as lovable, warm, and friendly in their advertisements. Generations later the image of Santa is much more cordial and the Coke magazine ads portraying him are nice collectibles.

Coke did their first advertising calender in 1891. The company calendar bore the name of owner Asa Chandler and assured that the product was "a delightful summer or winter drink. For headache, or tired feeling, relieves mental and physical exhaustion."

From the 1980s on, street cars or trolleys proved to be an excellent place to post not only Coca-Cola signs, but also the products

Cherry Smash bottle display, 1920s. Photo courtesy of Hake's Americana & Collectibles.

Coke advertising card, 1940s.

Swank *magazine ad promoting Coke, 1920s.*

Coke advertisement featuring Santa, from 1961 National Geographic.

and services of many other forward-thinking producers. The cost of reaching the traveler was low, and the milieu was convenient. The trolley was nearly the sole means of public transportation, and there was plenty of time for reading while on board. Eventually the trolley gave way to the public bus, subway, and shuttle—all of which in turn provided a place for various advertisements. Today there is a high regard for the early trolley signs, not only for the product but for their unique early mass-transportation usage.

Coke also used sports programs and schedules for printed advertising into the 1970s. Among their early newspaper ads, the series of baseball player promotions used by the D'arcy Company is one of the most popular. These particular ads first appeared around 1906 and continued in various newspapers for about ten years.

During the first 70 years of the century, this famous soft drink firm was undoubtedly

one of the most prolific advertisers on paper beyond magazines, signs, and newspapers. They used playing cards, trade cards, needle cases, coupons, festoons, bookmarks, ink blotters, early menus, sheet music, bumper stickers, and even cardboard cutout signs, including stand-up Santas during the 1960s.

Campbell Soup

Besides Coke, Campbell Soup Company is another leading example of a highly successful business extending itself into nearly every element of paper advertising, much to the joy of collectors.

This famous soup really had two beginnings as far as the collector is concerned. One was the development of the company itself in the late 1880s, and the other pertains to the role of legendary artist Grace Gebbie Drayton. As the story goes, the company, like Coca-Cola, had been using signs on street cars in the early 1900s. When comic strip artist Drayton married one of the workers at the shop that printed the advertising cards, a business connection between Campbell and

Drayton was established. One happy result was the full-cheeked Campbell Kids, which delighted trolley riders and have delighted others ever since. Drayton continued her contributions to Campbell Soup until her death in 1936. The colorful magazine advertisements featuring the Campbell Kids are probably the best known. However, postcards from 1912 and 1932 bearing the likeness of the Campbell Kids are worth considerably more, with values ranging from $30 to $70. The Campbell Kids can also be found on place mats, cookbooks, and other products manufactured in various amounts over the years.

During the cold, wintry month of January, Campbell still sells 100 cans of soup every second of every day. They sell 65 cans per second the rest of the year, so all that printed advertising must have paid off.

Morton Salt

Speaking of familiar images like Coke and the Campbell Kids, the girl in the Morton Salt ads has been clutching an umbrella and marching through the rain for some 80 years. She, too, is one of America's most recognized and collectible advertising symbols. This nation's eight-year-old girl next door has been the subject of striking magazine advertisements. However, she has also made quite a worldwide impression on everything else too, from trade cards, posters, and calendars to signs and ink blotters.

The Morton Salt girl, like many other advertising personae, got her start in magazine ads. A group of 12 ads and three alternatives were prepared for *Good Housekeeping* magazine in the early days of the salt company. One of the alternatives—depicting a curly-headed little girl holding an umbrella and a tilted package of salt—caught the eye of Sterling Morton, son of the company's president. The image suggested the phrase "When it rains it pours"—a play on words alluding to the fact that dampness would not hinder the flow from the container.

"Unlike Little Orphan Annie," commented a company source a few years ago, "the ageless Morton umbrella girl has been given a new wardrobe and hairstyle from time to time to keep her fashionable." Besides the various fashions, the umbrella itself also changed several times. Originally white, it was changed to blue in 1921 and then to yellow lined with white in 1956. Twelve years later it went back to white, this time lined with lavender.

Collectors can focus on particular fashions of the Morton Salt girl, umbrella variations, or the various types of Morton advertising and promotions. My own approach to this particular paper advertising collectible is quite personal. The 1920s and '30s Morton Girl with the pretty yellow dress and the ribbon in her hair was, to a large extent, my mother. In the early 1920s, artist Mary Anderson used her seven-year-old niece as a model for her commercial rendering. The studio for the famed drawing was the backyard of her home near the Ohio River. Miss Anderson, a professional artist, was well known at the time for commercial work using children as subjects. Her drawings frequently appeared on the covers of *Better Homes and Gardens, Playmate for Children,* and *McCall's.* Her talents ranged from book illustrations to penning some of the children of the Dutch Cleanser advertisements.

To the trained eye, there is a clear distinction among the various Morton girls, and there is likewise a close resemblance to one particular run of drawings and photographs of my mother at that age. During years of digging through this advertising memorabilia, I also uncovered one interesting fact. Although the company updated the Morton Salt girl over the years, they sometimes continued to use older images for ads and promotional purposes. The official Morton company line, understandably in terms of royalities and other financial claims, has been that everybody sees a resemblance to the figures and there never was an official model. In reality however, various free-lance commercial illustrators who directly contributed to the girl's changing composite did use models, often informally and always unofficially.

Fact Vs. Fiction

There is sometimes a fine line between the reality and the fiction of these advertising figures that have appeared so pleasingly for so long on paper. I once got involved in a controversy because of a nationally published article which pointed out that America's amazing Gold Dust Twins never really existed beyond the inspiration of a soap company executive and the imagination of a renowned artist. The drawing of two black children sitting in a washtub became a classic and was eventually depicted millions of times on scores of cleaning products and promotional premiums. The fictional twins were, in fact, one of the best known symbols in America at one time.

However, for all of that, the article was disputed by a reader of the publication who had documentation that his father was indeed one of the Gold Dust Twins. Actually, we were both right. The man's father had no doubt represented one of the fabled Gold Dust Twins and, perhaps, had paid been for his talents either directly by the company or through an agency. But in reality, he was still just dressed as a fictional figure with no true identity. The twins never actually existed anymore than the Morton Salt girl or Betty Crocker, even though the N.K. Fairbanks Soap Company of Chicago had live twins distributing promotional booklets at the St. Louis World's Fair in 1904.

Today, most any of the Gold Dust Twins material—soap boxes, magazine ads, cardboard signs, fans, and trade cards—are extremely popular with advertising collectors as well as those who acquire black memorabilia. The artwork for the Fairbanks figures was done by a leading artist of the time, Edward Windsor Kemble. Today the pen-and-ink drawings by Kemble, who died in 1933, fetch hundreds of dollars. Undoubtedly, original illustrations depicting the Gold Dust Twins

themselves would be worth thousands of dollars in the marketplace.

Packaging

Packaging, the colorful container that held the consumer product, is a relatively new arrival to paper advertising collecting, with interest extending from the Morton Salt cylinder containers to the dazzling display boxes for trading cards.

Back in the late 1940s, the Lone Ranger's radio listeners were given the opportunity to own the masked man's Frontier Town. The price, four *Cheerios* box tops and four dimes, was relatively high for most fans at the time, but it would entitle them to the whole cardboard town. The price of a seven-ounce box was 18 cents but included one box top and three wild west models which could be cut out from the back of the package. Very few children could afford the premium, and hardly anyone saved cereal boxes in those

Colonel Morton, trademark character of Morton Frozen Pies, punch-out mask and badge, 1950s. Photo courtesy of Hake's Americana & Collectibles.

The Little Turk, Scott's Emulsion, trade card, ca. 1900.

Clermont Cooking Stoves trade card, 1890s.

days. The result is that the Lone Ranger's Frontier Town is probably the most prized radio premium in history.

Boxes of Wheaties cereal are not an unusual collectible today, but they once were. Wheaties was one of the first breakfast foods associated with premium offers in exchange for box tops, and in 1933, the producer began what would become a legendary association with athletes. By 1939 the company had signed 46 of the 51 baseball players selected for the first major league all-star game to promote the breakfast of champions. Their baseball heroes have included all the great players from Babe Ruth to Pete Rose, and their range of other athletes has extended from animal trainer Maria Rasputin to gymnast Mary Lou Retton.

Trade Cards

One of America's earliest forms of printed advertising, other than colonial newspapers and almanacs, was advertising or trade cards. They were a useful medium from the early 1800s to the early 1900s and probably enjoyed their greatest glory in the Victorian era of the 1890s. As brand names began to have impact, there was a significant tendency to portray a domestic setting of a family, children, or dogs. Sometimes the images bore a relationship to the product, but just as often they were simply there to appeal to members of the household and to mirror, if possible, the typical middle-class lifestyle.

The golden era of trade cards, just prior to the 20th century, came about in part because of new technology which allowed li-

Mrs. Winslows Soothing Syrup trade card, 1888.

Cigarette trade card, W. Duke Sons & Co., late 19th century.

thography and color printing to be done relatively inexpensively. Just as important, if not more so, was the emerging art of product advertising. Americans in all regions of the country, with little to read and even less in terms of colorful illustrations, became a perfect market for the trade cards.

Beggar children were featured on Jayne's Expectorant trade card of 1890. On the back side of the card was the message, "Illustrating types of poverty which never fail to appeal, all the world over, to the kindliest feelings of our human nature." Arbuckle Coffee Company, one of the first firms to insert premium trade cards with their product to promote sales, issued a single 50-card set of children, animals, and historical events. Later the McLaughlin Coffee Company bested that with 225 different cards of children's daily activities.

Victorian adults and children often collected the various trade cards and pasted them in ornate scrapbooks. Today, a century later, the scrapbooks themselves are a prime source of the collectible advertising cards. Many remain in the marketplace at affordable prices, while still others are still to be discovered in closeted collections of advertising paper.

Almanacs

Advertising almanacs, an intriguing area of paper collectibles, not only predate trade cards but postdate them as well. Almanacs have been around since the late 1600s, although commercial sponsorship and the advertising aspect came much later. By the 1890s millions of patent-machine almanacs were being distributed every year to a semirural population that loved them. For

Animal card, Arbuckle Brothers Coffee, 1890.
Photo courtesy of Hake's Americana & Collectibles.

Persia country card, Arbuckle Brothers Coffee,
1889. Photo courtesy of Hake's Americana & Collectibles.

Gorilla animal card, Arbuckle Brothers Coffee,
1890. Photo courtesy of Hake's Americana & Collectibles.

Trade card, Gold Band Coffee, Columbus's voyage, 1890s.

Venezuela country card, Arbuckle Brothers Coffee,
1889. Photo courtesy of Hake's Americana & Collectibles.

many families *Dr. Morse's Indian Root Pills Almanac*, a drugstore giveaway during the turn of the century, was the only book they could afford. Various almanacs with commercial connections such as *Kellogg's Housewife Almanac Yearbook*, *B.F. Goodrich Farmer's Handbook and Almanac*, and

Horlick's Malted Milk, issued through radio's Lum and Abner, were around through the 1950s.

Automobiles

A final comment on automobile advertisements and prints. Those starting in the early 1900s and running through the 1920s and 1930s are especially collectible. Similar ads from the 1950s and 1960s cannot be far behind. Road maps at reasonable rates have a growing number of collectors, but instruction books and service manuals may prove to be one of the true treasures of paper advertising. The best of the best are the showroom catalogs with all the glorious, detailed information on models and options. Today they are generally hard to find, even from as recently as the 1970s.

During the 1980s one of the country's leading collectors and dealers in automobilia literature, much of it advertising related, was Walter Miller of Syracuse, New York. In 1987 he was reported to have one million pieces of auto literature, the largest private collection in the world. "This is definitely an avocation I turned into a vocation," he once told a journalist. "When I started collecting auto advertisements from old magazines when I was a boy, I had no idea it would turn into this." Walter Miller's Antique Car Literature became a business that eventually employed eight people, with customers in 100 countries.

Miller was quoted as saying that people who were interested in this type of material fell into two general categories: the hard-core enthusiasts who collect just the literature, and the owner of a special car who wants all the literature that pertains to that particular vehicle. Price is not the problem for collectors at the level either, Miller felt, "especially given that some of that literature is downright obscure. Take the 1930 Packard catalog, for instance. I have a dozen loyal customers waiting for the next one I find."

RECOMMENDED READING

Hake's Guide to Advertising Collectibles by Ted Hake, Wallace-Homestead.

Huxford's Collectible Advertising Value Guide by Sharon and Bob Huxford, Collector Books.

Advertising Identification and Price Guide by Dawn Reno, Confident Collector Series, Avon Books.

America's Best-Loved Foods, I'm A Spam Fan by Carolyn Wyman, Longmeadow Press.

PRICE LISTINGS

Almanac, Rexall Drugs, 1941, $4

Almanac, radio premium, Horlick's Malted Milk Corp., 1936, Lum and Abner, 34 pages, $35

Automobile catalog, Chevrolet, 1964, 12-page glossy publication, full color, 11 × 13, $22

Automobile catalog, Ford Motor Company, 1927, models in full color, 12 pages, 6 × 8, $45

Automobile catalog sheet, LaFayette automobile, 1935, four-model folder, 19 × 22, $60

Automobile preview catalog, General Motors, 1954, includes Chevrolet, Pontiac, Buick, Cadillac, 16 pages, black-and-white photos, stiff paper, 6 × 9, $36

1939 Silver Streak Pontiac catalog. Photo courtesy of Hake's Americana & Collectibles.

Chevrolet catalog, full color, 1964. Photo courtesy of Hake's Americana & Collectibles.

1935 LaFayette catalog sheet, folder shows four autos built by Nash. Photo courtesy of Hake's Americana & Collectibles.

Preview booklet, GM cars, 1954. Photo courtesy of Hake's Americana & Collectibles.

Bottle display, Cherry Smash, die cut, full color, boy in patriotic outfit, 1920s, 7.5 × 11.5, $35

Calendar, desk, premium, Tydol Gasoline and Veedol Oil, 1954, unused, 4 × 6, $28

Calendar, wall, Keystone Emery with Miss Liberty, 1943, full-color portrait, 9 × 13, $55

Tydol Gasoline/Veedol Oil calendar, December 1954 through December 1955. Photo courtesy of Hake's Americana & Collectibles.

Pinup calendar, "Spirit of Liberty," 1943. Photo courtesy of Hake's Americana & Collectibles.

Catalog, binoculars, and accessories, Bausch & Lomb, 1948, with prices, 32 pages, 9 × 6, $30

Check, Dickson Coca-Cola Bottling Company, Coke logo, 1921, Dickson, Tennessee, $15

Cigarette advertising poster, Raleigh, 1940s, 12 × 18, $60

Flyer, Great Northern Railroad, 1926, Columbia River expedition/celebration, black and white, 9 × 12, $22

Individual endorsement ad, Lucky Strike Cigarettes with Amelia Earhart, 1928 magazine ad, $55

Ink blotter advertisement, Coke, 1940s, with carton and child, full color, $5

Ink blotter advertisement, White Flash Motor Oil, lot of three, ca. 1930s, full color, 3 × 6, $28

Label, citrus crate, Turnbill, ca. 1930s, Indian rowing, 9 × 9, $7

Label, fruit crate, Statue brand, bartletts, $6

Label, liquor, Old Black Joe brand, dry gin, ca. 1930s, $3

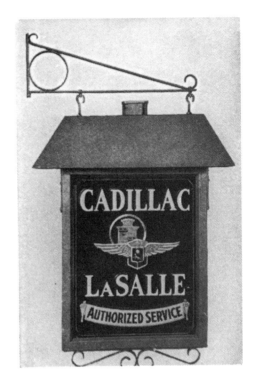

Old Black Joe gin label, 1930s.

LA SALLE OPERATOR'S MANUAL

1. **For the first 500 miles** drive the car at moderate speeds.

2. **Operate the car** in accordance with the instructions contained in this manual.

3. **Check the Engine oil level** every 100 to 150 miles and add oil as often as necessary to keep the indicator at "full"

4. **Check the tire pressure** at least once a week and keep it up to the recommended pressure—25 pounds front and 30 pounds rear.

5. **Add distilled water to the storage battery** every 1000 miles, and in warm weather every 500 miles, or at least every two weeks.

6. **Lubricate the car** every 1000 miles or once a month in accordance with the lubrication schedule and chart.

7. **Have the car inspected** by an authorized Cadillac-La Salle Service Station every 1000 miles or once a month.

Keep this Manual in the Instrument Panel Package Compartment.

1934 LaSalle operator's manual, auto produced by Cadillac division. Photos courtesy of Hake's Americana & Collectibles.

Advertisement, Disney hats, from Walt Disney Magazine, 1957. *Photo courtesy of Hake's Americana & Collectibles.*

Magazine advertisement, Morton Salt girls, six types, *Time* magazine, 1969, full-color, $6

Newspaper advertisement, Quaker Wheat Crackles, heavyweight boxing champion Max Baer, physical-development set premium, 1935, full color, $22

Owner's manual, LaSalle, 1934, produced by Cadillac division, 54 pages, 5 × 7, $32

"Tydol Trails Thru Pennsylvania" map, 1936. Photo courtesy of Hake's Americana & Collectibles.

New-Value Dodge! *promotional newspaper for introduction of 1935 Dodge. Photo courtesy of Hake's Americana & Collectibles.*

Page advertisement, *Walt Disney Magazine,* 1957, for Disney hats, includes Mousketeer hat, black and white, $8

Postcard, Rice Krispies, 1952, Snap, Crackle and Pop, full-color, Battle Creek, Michigan, $7.50

Postcard, Goodyear Tire dealer, 1930s, 1¢ postage, $10

Premium promotion, Colonel Morton punch-out mask and badge, Morton Frozen Pies, ca. 1950s, full color, $25

Premium poster, Coca-Cola and Burger Chef, 1977, Star Wars, 18 × 24, $20

Promotional booklet, *Fifty Years of Woolworth,* 1929, good condition, 48 pages, $30

Promotional newspaper, *New Value Dodge,* 1935, eight pages, Dodge autos, 9 × 12, $35

Road map, Tydol Oil Company, 1936, "Tydol Trails through Pennsylvania," 4 × 9, $15

Store sign, Ralston cereal, 1933, Tom Mix radio program, cardboard, 14 × 23, $500

Soft drink six-pack carton, Squirt, 1960s, three colors, $4

Sports advertising card, Babe Ruth for Blue Bird beverage, ca. 1935, mint, 5 × 7, $600

Tobacco advertising poster, Granger tobacco, 1940s, 14 × 20, $35

Tobacco label from package, Rudolph Valentino picture and facsimile signature, ca. 1920, $80

Tobacco poster, Bravo brand with bull fighter, 1890s, full color, 6 × 8, $20

Toy catalog, Cook Toys, 1960, includes Barbie, Lone Ranger, Ideal, Hanna-Barbera items, 32 pages, full color, 8 × 11, $65

Trade card, Scott's Emulsion, Little Turk, 1890s, full color, $8

Trade card, Clark's O.N.T. Thread, 1890s, with children, $5

Trolley advertising card, Centaur Liniment, ca. 1890s, full color, 13 × 6.5, $25

Trolley advertising card, J.M. & I. Railroad, three colors, 14 × 7.5, $22

Centaur Liniment advertising poster card, 1890s.

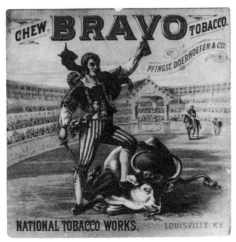

Bravo Tobacco advertising poster, full color, 1890s.

Railroad poster card, 1890s.

ENTERTAINMENT

Sheet Music

Al Smith would not normally be on anyone's list of entertainers. Smith's real claim to fame, aside from being governor of New York, was losing the presidential election to Herbert Hoover in 1928. In fact, it was Smith, not Hoover, who used the famous phrase "a chicken in every pot." Although Smith was a politician he was known to have sung some songs from time to time. His official campaign song, "The Sidewalks of New York," lived on for decades after the election.

A few years ago my wife and I were spending a rainy Saturday afternoon at a nearby antiques mall when we spotted a copy of the sheet music for "Sidewalks of New York." Even more exciting was the fact that it bore the photograph of Al Smith on the cover and was identified as his official campaign song. The sheet music was bound in plastic, but since it was clearly a good buy at $4, we didn't bother to have it removed.

Once at home we discovered the cardboard backing held some additional treasures: an autographed glossy, black-and-white photograph of Al Smith and a letter to an eight-year-old girl who had written him to ask for the signed photograph. The letter was dated November 1928 shortly after the presidential election.

The moral of the story, and this book, is that there still are some great finds to be discovered, whether in the local antiques mall, your neighbor's garage sale, or one of the country's leading antiques and paper collectibles shows.

As far as presidential candidates and sheet music are concerned, they go together. After George Washington, every presidential candidate—winners and losers—was championed with at least one campaign song and the sheet music that went with it. Such things, even those from the 20th century, would make a nice collection today. During the mid-

"The Sidewalks of New York" sheet music, official Al Smith campaign issue, 1928.

Cotton Club Parade promotional sheet music.

dle of this century, Irvin Berlin wrote "They Like Ike" for his hit musical *Call Me Madam,* and a few years later it became the campaign song for Dwight Eisenhower. John Kennedy even had a campaign song with sheet music. However, it is little known and considered rare today (see political section).

In the early 1990s one of the most impressive overall collections of sheet music this century has ever seen went from the hands of a private collector to the Smithsonian Institution. The collection contained not only the printed works of George Gershwin, Irving Berlin, and Cole Porter, but George M. Cohan's patriotic classic, "Over There," with illustrations by Norman Rockwell. The curator of American music at the Smithsonian commented at the time, "This is one of the great, legendary collections of sheet music in the world."

One reason acquiring the collection attracted so much national attention was the renewed interest in sheet music of the past. Besides all the reasons it was appreciated before, today's collectors view it as decorative art as well as collectible, and colorful sheets are now framed and hung on walls. Millions of viewers saw exactly that a few years ago when *60 Minutes* interviewed legendary entertainer Whoopi Goldberg in her Victorian home in New England.

Millions of song sheets were printed during the glory days of the technique, attracting the skills of such artists as Palmer Cox, Harrison Fisher, James Montgomery Flagg, Nathaniel Currier, E.H. Pfeiffer, and Grace Drayton. Today each of those artists has a following of collectors.

Various wars also spawned patriotic songs —from the Civil War's "When Johnny Comes Marching Home" to the tune popularized by Jimmy Dorsey's orchestra in World War II, "Comin' In on a Wing and a Prayer"—and some collectors specialize in this subject. Collectors of black memorabilia also have a significant interest in some sheet music, and some song sheets have a higher value as black memorabilia than in any other market. The world of Disney, too, extends

Sheet music from 1939 World's Fair, "A World's Fair Waltz."

into sheet music as it does in so many other collectible fields. Lovely Disney songs from the 1940s, e.g., "A Dream is a Wish Your Heart Makes" from Cinderella and "When You Wish Upon a Star" from Pinocchio, will always be wonderful collectibles.

Disneyana

Of course, there is much more to Disney entertainment paper than sheet music or even those fantastic movie posters from original releases and re-releases. In the spring of 1993 Swann Galleries sold what may have been the most unique collection of Disney on paper. Going to the highest bidder were 2,800 daily Mickey Mouse comic strips, each painstakingly removed from a Milwaukee newspaper during the 1930s. This virtually complete assemblage of Mickey comic strips brought $2,640.

The works and characters of the great Walt Disney on paper, from comic strips to trading cards, span more than 60 years, and for the collector much of it is quite affordable.

During the same "comic strip" auction, Swann's sold a copy of *The Adventures of Mickey Mouse Book One* by Philadelphia publisher David McKay. The 1931 edition brought $825, but later editions often appear in the marketplace for much less. In recent years Hake's Americana & Collectibles sold a 1942 get-well card depicting Mickey Mouse as a surgeon near a hospital sign reading, "We cure everything but bacon." It brought $25.

Disney movie posters of the late 1940s are, of course, among the classic paper collectibles of the 20th century and command thousands of dollars at leading auctions and other collector outlets. However, the more recent re-releases are more abundant and affordable. Video sales and rentals in the past ten years have provided still another source of colorful Disney posters.

Starting in 1944, Disney characters filled the pages of Little Golden Books. The first two, *Through the Picture Frame* and *The Cold Blooded Penguin,* both by Robert Edmunds, are hard to find. However, other late-1940s classics, such as *Snow White, Dumbo, Peter and the Wolf,* and *Uncle Remus,* remain available. Little Golden Book titles from the 1950s, such as *Bongo, Three Little Pigs, Cinderella, The Ugly Duckling,* and *Mickey Mouse and the Pluto Pup,* often still list from $3 to $12 in good condition. Many TV-related Disney books from the Little Golden series of the late 1950s and early 1960s, like *Davy Crockett* and *Zorro,* often are priced somewhat higher.

Magazines have also long been a good medium for Disneyana. Nice copies of the Mickey Mouse magazines from the 1930s, complete with color comics, often bring $75 or more. The British versions from the same era usually sell for about half the price of American editions. Mickey Mouse Club magazines from the 1950s, as well as club annuals, often list at $20 to $40 and make very colorful collectibles.

While a pocket-sized Donald Duck comic book from a box of 1940s breakfast cereal may run well over $100 today, there is a wealth of Disney paper, including calendars, decals, and children's books, which can be collected for much less. Sometimes overlooked are the dandy Disney record albums, which are quite attractive and decorative. A Disney 45-rpm record album of the 1949 "The Grasshopper and the Ants" runs $15 to $25. The Disney record album from the 1973 Robin Hood cartoon feature, complete with 11-page booklet, is $6 to $8.

Record Album Covers

Record albums have considerable merit when it comes to paper collectibles in the entertainment field. For nearly 60 years Americans enjoyed playing music on flat records, first rubber and later vinyl. In the late 1940s Columbia Records came up with long-playing or LP records. The 33-rpm records were wider and more durable than the older 78s, and, more importantly, they arrived coincidentally with the inauguration of charming and colorful record-album covers. The covers were eye-catching and, consequently, became a major part of record marketing into the 1970s. By the middle 1970s flat records were giving way to audio cassettes, and the

The Story of Star Wars sound-track album, 1977. *Photo courtesy of Hake's Americana & Collectibles.*

1980s saw the dramatic onset of CDs or compact disc recordings. As a practical marketing matter, LP albums are gone forever, but as a decorator item and a collectible, the covers are just coming into their own.

Cowboy Heroes

You can find cowboy heroes like Gene Autry and Roy Rogers on record albums, and you can find them on just about everything else, too. These six-gun champions did not ride out of the Old West as much as they arose from radio, movies, and television. Today they are legends.

Hopalong Cassidy made the jump from movies to the TV screen in 1948 and was fortunate enough to bring a collection of his old movies with him. When Gene and Roy followed a few years later, they ended up with made-for-TV shows. All of them left a great number of paper products in their wake, ranging from story books to coloring books.

During the second half of the 1950s, another dimension arrived in cowboy-hero merchandising—Western stars who were no longer crossovers from another medium but were original to TV shows. By 1959 there were more than 30 different Western series running on television, which in turn led to a vast quantity of related merchandise, usually produced in much smaller amounts than those for the "big three," but colorful contributions nevertheless.

As late as 1965, the Sears spring and summer catalog still listed Roy Rogers and Dale Evans outfits. Each three-piece set with shirt, pants, and belt was priced at $5.97. Today, even the catalogs which carried the information are prized.

Coloring Books

Cowboy stars appeared in coloring books for many years and so did just about every cartoon character and TV hero of this century. While collecting coloring books by themselves is relatively new in the paper collectibles field, collecting them in connection with a particular personality has been a hobby for a long time. Collectors of Roy Rogers memorabilia will undoubtedly want a coloring book or two, as will fans of Mickey Mouse or *Leave It To Beaver*.

The vast majority of coloring books produced in this country came from a few very distinguished publishing firms, starting with McLoughlin Brothers and later including Saalfield, Whitman, Lowe, Abbot, and Merrill Publishing.

Television shows like *Leave It to Beaver* were far and away the dominant theme for coloring books during the late 1950s and early 1960s. Nearly every major network show accounted for at least one. Among the cast of TV shows with collectible books are *Beany & Cecil, Flintstones, Atom Ant, Pixie & Dixie, Green Acres, Julia* (with Diahann Carroll), *Daniel Boone* (with Fess Parker), *Addams Family, Batman, Car 55, Where Are You?,* and *Superman*.

Comic and cartoon characters ready to be colored in the 1960s included the likes of Dennis the Menace, Beetle Bailey, Alley Oop, Casper, Tom and Jerry, and King Leonard.

World's Fairs

World's Fairs have been one of the most enduring providers of entertainment-based paper collectibles. People have carried home, saved, and passed on Fair material for well over a century. In the 1980s a Florida senior citizen built an entire museum dedicated to collectibles from the 1933 Chicago World's Fair. His homemade museum housed 2,000 pieces including tickets, posters, photographs, and brochures. Today, posters, programs, and playing cards from the many World's Fairs continue to be seasoned collectibles.

Rock concerts and their memorabilia are about as new to paper collecting as Fairs are old. Programs, tickets, posters, decals, and the like really began showing up on the collectibles scene in the early 1990s. Now major magazines regularly carry advertisements and prices for choice items. It undoubtedly will be a far-reaching collecting field.

Official poster of 1933 World's Fair, Chicago, red,
white, and blue.

Screen Romances *magazine, Jean Harlow cover,
November 1933. Photo courtesy of Hake's Americana & Collectibles.*

Poster for Universal Exposition, Paris, 1889.
Photo courtesy of Swann Galleries, Inc.

Screen Romances *magazine, Jean Harlow cover,
August 1934. Photo courtesy of Hake's Americana
& Collectibles.*

Fan Magazines

Magazines of the past have a rich future with collectors. Most highly prized are fan magazines because older Americans realize they have disappeared and many younger Americans have grown up never really seeing them in the mailbox or on the newsstand. Fan magazines prospered during the Great Depression of the 1930s and were one of the few things that remained available during the grim days of World War II. During the 1930s most of the covers were devoted to female stars of the screen like Claudette Colbert, Ginger Rogers, and Jean Harlow, but in the 1940s, male stars like Van Johnson and Clark Gable got just as much front-page coverage. More than two dozen fan magazines were still going strong into the 1950s with a collective readership of over 12 million. *Photoplay*

Personal Story *magazine, Gina Lollobrigida cover, 1955. Photo courtesy of Hake's Americana & Collectibles.*

Motion Picture *magazines from the 1940s, Clark Gable and Ann Sheridan. Photo courtesy of Hake's Americana & Collectibles.*

Motion Picture *magazines from the 1940s. Photo courtesy of Hake's Americana & Collectibles.*

alone had a monthly circulation of more than one million.

The dazzling impact of television had a profoundly diminishing effect on movies and their fan magazines. Some of the fan magazines turned to TV and their stars, while others just faded away. As fan magazines began to dwindle, the country saw a brief rise in alternative scandal magazines. *Inside Story, Uncensored, Confidential,* and *Hush-Hush* were very sensational for their time in the late 1950s and early 1960s, often bordering on the totally irresponsible. Today, like their fan-magazine cousins, they are an interesting collectible from the entertainment field.

Movie Memorabilia

Movies are, of course, the biggest element of entertainment collectibles, and the field continues to grow and expand particularly in respect to paper items. One reason is the multitude of television channels available to a majority of Americans and the home videos accessible to almost everyone. One way or another, all the classic and the not-so-classic—even the obscure—films of previous generations are readily available. As a result, pictures, posters, and related promotions have eternal life.

Another factor is the new wave of Hollywood motion-picture marketing that gives audiences new encounters with the likes of past heroes such as Batman, Superman, and Dick Tracy. In 1989 Walt Disney allocated a then-record $48.1 million for the publicity budget of the Dick Tracy movie. Not only does such marketing revise and revitalize prior Dick Tracy material, but it also opens a vast marketplace or new memorabilia, from bookmarks to special issue magazines.

Posters continue to be produced for the estimated 250 films produced each year in this country. (Actually the U.S. is in third

Tangier Incident *movie poster, starring George Brent, 1953. Photo courtesy of Hake's Americana & Collectibles.*

The Eternal Sea *movie poster, 1953. Photo courtesy of Hake's Americana & Collectibles.*

place behind Japan with 300 plus annually and India with a staggering 800 per year.) Many of the movies go on to the video market with a further production of multicolored posters.

Meanwhile, lobby cards or scene cards, usually smaller than posters and on stiffer paper, have not been produced in any significant numbers since the 1960s. Many are still available in the marketplace at reasonable prices. On the other hand, movie stills are still being produced by movie companies and continue to be attractive collectibles. The stills, usually scenes from the film, are sometimes used instead of lobby cards at movie houses and are always used as promotions to be dispatched with press kits. Among the black-and-white, glossy stills, sex symbols of the silver screen are likely the most popular,

Jaguar *movie poster, starring Sabu, 1955. Photo courtesy of Hake's Americana & Collectibles.*

Irma La Douce *movie card, 1963. Photo courtesy of Hake's Americana & Collectibles.*

Paris When It Sizzles *movie card, 1964. Photo courtesy of Hake's Americana & Collectibles.*

Lolita *lobby card, MGM Seven Arts film, 1962. Photo courtesy of Hake's Americana & Collectibles.*

followed by horror films, B westerns, and mid-20th-century musicals.

Paper collectibles dealing with entertainment can provide a few shaggy dog stories too. In January of 1994, Swann Galleries con-ducted a major auction of Joan Crawford memorabilia. Included in the fantastic material, much of which was the original property of the famed screen actress, was but a single dog-related item.

A typed letter from the El Rancho Rin-Tin-Tin ranch did not even rate a mention in the New York auction gallery's advance press release on the sale, even though it included the stamp-inked paw prints of both Rin-Tin-Tin I and Rin-Tin-Tin IV. The typed letter, dated October 29, 1956, and signed by Lee Duncan, along with the separate sheet of prints, were described in Swann's catalog as being "both on amusing letterhead of El Rancho." The presale estimate on the canine correspondence was $80 to $120. On the day of the Joan Crawford memorabilia sale, it brought a startling $1,093.

Still from Columbia movie serial, 1949.

Other paper items from Hollywood include souvenir magazines—those similar to fan magazines but centering on a single film. They are still being produced and have a good collectible future. Also worth considering are book novelizations from movies, books about the "making of" a particular movie, and original film scripts.

As with all other paper collectibles, condition is important with entertainment memorabilia. *Chicago Tribune* movie critic Dave Kehr once wrote of finding a movie poster in a musty old bookstore in his youth. It happened to be a 1950s poster of the original *Invasion of the Body Snatchers,* but it was slightly damaged. "How much for it?", he asked the store's owner. "One dollar," was the reply. "In this shape," challenged the youngster. "Well," answered the annoyed shopkeeper as he tore the poster to pieces and let it drop to the floor," "How about this shape?"

RECOMMENDED READING

Official Identification and Price Guide to Movie Memorabilia by Richard DeThuin, House of Collectibles.

Goldmine's Price Guide to Collectible Record Albums, 3rd edition, by Neal Umphred, Krause Publications.

Official Price Guide to Rock and Roll Magazines, Posters and Memorabilia by David Henkel, House of Collectibles.

Collector's Guide to Treasures From the Silver Screen by John Hegenberger, Wallace-Homestead.

The Sheet Music Reference & Price Guide by Anna Guiheen and Marie-Reine Pafik, Collector Books.

Collectible Coloring Books by Dian Zillner, Collector Books.

PRICE LISTINGS

Album cover and record, "Wyatt Earp, Western Marshall," 1958, 45 rpm, Peter Pan label, $15

Album cover and record, "Walt Disney's Animated Robin Hood," 1973, 33 rpm, with 11-page booklet, $8

Album cover and record, signed Alice Cooper, "Welcome to My Nightmare," $125

Pinocchio *book, Whitman Co., 1939. Photo courtesy of Hake's Americana & Collectibles.*

Children's book, *Pinocchio,* 1939,
Whitman Publishing, 48 pages, $55

Children's book, *Tales of Wells Fargo,*
1958, Little Golden Book, 24 pages,
$20

Children's book, *Zorro,* 1958, Golden
Press, softcover, $18

Circus ticket, Ringling Brothers, 1933,
50th anniversary show, $8

Coloring book, *Hopalong Cassidy,* 1950,
Abbot Publishing Company, 20 pages,
$60

Coloring book, *Leave It to Beaver,* 1958,
Saalfield Publishing, $85

Coloring book, *Hee Haw* TV show,
1970, Saalfield Publishing, $55

Coloring book, *Mackenzie's Raiders,*
1960, Saalfield Publishing, 96 pages,
$30

Comic book, *Star Wars Weekly,* 1978,
English, Marvel Comics International,
20 pages, $32

Hopalong, startled and alert, calls out to Lucky, "There's trouble
ahead—do you smell it?"

Hopalong Cassidy *coloring book, Abbot Publishing Co., ca. 1950. Photo courtesy of Hake's Americana & Collectibles.*

Concert ticket, unused, Pink Floyd,
1977, Anaheim Stadium, Animals
tour, $30

Walt Disney's Zorro, *softcover book, Golden Press, 1958. Photo courtesy of Hake's Americana & Collectibles.*

Mackenzie's Raiders *coloring book, 1960. Photo courtesy of Hake's Americana & Collectibles.*

Star Wars Weekly, *English comic book, 1978.*
Photo courtesy of Hake's Americana & Collecti-
bles.

Concert ticket, unused, Rolling Stones,
   1981, Candlestick Park, San
   Francisco, Tattoo You tour, $35

Concert ticket stub, Eric Clapton, 1975,
   Tampa Stadium, Florida, $18

Exhibit card, Monkees, 1966,
   promotional item, $4

Hardcover movie book, *Hollywood
   Babylon,* 1975, Jayne Mansfield on
   jacket, mint, $20

Guide, Disneyland, 1962, Walt Disney
   cover, $35

Guidebook, World's Fair, 1939, New
   York, 256 pages, $40

Lobby cards, *Above Suspicion,* 1943, set
   of eight, Loew's for MGM, $150

Lobby card, *April in Paris,* 1952, Doris
   Day and Ray Bolger, $15

Magazine, *Life,* 1945, Jimmy Stewart
   cover, $10

Magazine, *Screen Thrills Illustrated,*
   August 1964, pictorial quarterly, $22

Old Yeller and Tommy Kirk on cover of Walt
Disney Magazine, *1957. Photo courtesy of Hake's*
Americana & Collectibles.

Popular Screen, Jean Harlow cover, September
1934. Photo courtesy of Hake's Americana & Col-
lectibles.

Magazine, *TV Guide,* 1965, Andy Griffith cover, $15

Magazine, *Walt Disney Magazine,* 1957, Tommy Kirk and Old Yeller cover, $20

Magazine, *Personal Story,* first issue, June 1955, Gina Lollobrigida cover, $12

Magazine, *Popular Screen,* September 1937, Jean Harlow cover, full color, $40

Magazine, *Movie Life,* August 1943, Clark Gable cover, $20

Magazine, *Rolling Stone,* September 1977, Elvis cover, mint, $20

Magazine, *TV World,* June 1953, Lucille Ball cover, $10

Magazine, *Quick,* June 1952, Ruth Roman cover, $5

Magazine, *See,* July 1955, Marilyn Monroe cover, $35

Movie broadside, pulp paper, *Texas Renegades,* 1940, Tim McCoy, 9 × 12, $10

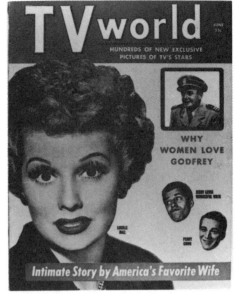

TV World *magazine, Lucille Ball cover, June 1953.*

Movie broadside, pulp paper, *The Vigilantes Ride,* 1940s, Russell Hayden, 6 × 8, $8

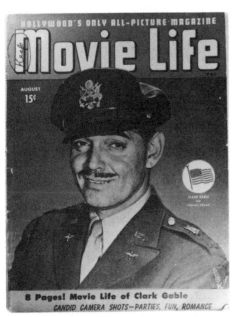

Movie Life *magazine, Clark Gable cover, August 1943.*

Quick *magazine, Ruth Roman cover, 1952.*

See magazine, Marilyn Monroe cover, July 1955. Photo courtesy of Hake's Americana & Collectibles.

Movie poster, *Charro,* 1969, Elvis Presley, full color, 30 × 40, $70

Movie poster, *Sands of Iwo Jima,* 1950, John Wayne, 9 × 14, $100

Movie poster, *Three Young Texans,* 1954, Jeffrey Hunter and Mitzi Gaynor, 11 × 14, $18

Paper dolls, booklet, John Wayne, 1981, doll figures and clothes, mint, $9

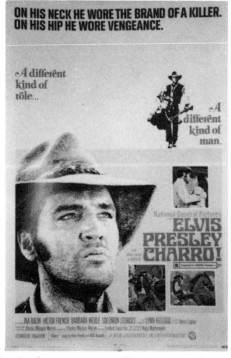

Elvis Presley movie poster, Charro!, *1969. Photo courtesy of Hake's Americana & Collectibles.*

John Wayne movie poster, Sands of Iwo Jima, *1950. Photo courtesy of Hake's Americana & Collectibles.*

Paper dolls, booklet, Gilda Radner, 1979, Avon Books, 12 pages, $28

Picture book, *The Wizard of Oz,* 1939, Bobbs-Merrill Company, 8 pages, $64

Playing cards, Green Hornet, 1965, mint in box, $23

Press book, *Dracula Has Risen From the Grave,* 1969, with Christopher Lee, $5

Pulp magazine, *The Shadow,* 1943, fair condition, $32

Pulp magazine, *The Spider,* August 1937, art cover, fine condition, $80

Reels and packet, View-Master, 1955, *Tarzan of the Apes,* $25

Reels and packet, View-Master, 1977, *Welcome Back, Kotter,* $25

Reels and packet, View-Master, 1977, John Travolta cover, $25

Sheet music, "April Love," 1957, Shirley Jones and Pat Boone, $5

Welcome Back, Kotter *View-Master reel envelope, 1977. Photo courtesy of Hake's Americana & Collectibles.*

Sheet music, "On the Good Ship Lollipop, 1934, from the movie *Bright Eyes* with Shirley Temple, $34

Sheet music, "A Dream is A Wish Your Heart Makes," 1949, from the movie *Cinderella,* Walt Disney, $10

Sheet music, "The Mighty Mo," 1952, aerial photo of battleship *Missouri,* $12

Travel brochure, Jasper National Park, 1938, Canada, foldout map, 45 pages, $15

HOLIDAYS

Halloween

When I was a youngster my sister frequently pointed out to me that the only holiday I was ever interested in was my own birthday. Over the years I matured to the point where Halloween and Groundhog's Day are my favorites.

When it comes to Halloween, I am not alone. Over the last decade in the United States, its collectibles have become second only to those of Christmas. Even in the early 1980s the idea of collecting paper things of past Christmas holidays was fairly new, and most other holidays were simply lumped to-

Wizard of Oz *picture book, Bobbs-Merrill Co., 1939. Photo courtesy of Hake's Americana & Collectibles.*

gether collectively as also-rans. Of course, that was at a time when outside Christmas decorations were popular but most other holidays (not counting the Fourth of July) were celebrated indoors. In the new wave of the 1990s, countless houses are decorated for Halloween and many are regularly decorated on the outside for Easter as well. When you see the first house decorations for Groundhog's Day go up in your neighborhood, remember where you read it first.

What helped Halloween collectibles move up from the pack, in my opinion, is that so many of them were stored away after the season and the holiday is such a child-related experience. Even families of modest means usually managed to get the children costumed for trick-or-treat night, and much of the decorations and other material were then carefully packed away—like Christmas tree ornaments—until the next year. This was rarely true of holiday trimmings in most households.

In some ways, Halloween leads the pack in terms of paper items produced—all potential collectibles. Consider paper cups, paper plates, prints, paper tablecloths, table decorations, trick or treat bags, tally cards, party invitations, place cards, crepe-paper streamers, and wall decorations. Material which is still in its original packaging is especially prized. The same laundry list, of course, applies to Christmas, New Year's Day, Valentine's Day, and all the rest, but, typically, there has been less of it to go around.

Halloween became firmly established in the American culture by the turn of the century and was an especially appealing topic on colorful postcards. From the early 1900s to the 1930s, a great number of these cards and other paper items featured some form of a jack-o'-lantern in deference to the superstition suggesting that they can drive away evil spirits lurking in the evening darkness.

Christmas

Historically, and also in terms of paper collectibles, Christmas had a much earlier start in the U.S. (as did Valentine's Day). In fact, they were the only two holidays for which greeting cards could actually be purchased in any significant number in retail stores in the 19th century. Some sources suggest a foldout nativity scene Christmas card was produced as early as 1820, but most experts cite Calcott Hoursley and the 1840s Royal Academy in England as being responsible for the first true group of Christmas cards. Acting upon the request of Henry Cole, who wanted to remember his friends during the holiday, the Academy produced cards, which were lithographed, hand colored, and marked "Summerly's Home Treasury Office, London." In 1843 they sold about 1,000 to the public at one shilling each, and soon other London publishers found the idea worthwhile. By the 1860s there were several English Christmas greeting card publishers.

Meanwhile in the U.S., Louis Prang founded a publishing firm after the Civil War, and by the 1870s he had perfected a rather advanced lithographic process of multicolor printing, which he called *Chromos*. He was soon producing engraved Christmas cards at Roxbury, Massachusetts, and having them shipped to England to meet the demand. Typically, the Prang cards of the 1870s and 1880s, which were fairly small and square-shaped, depicted floral designs or children, and bore simple messages wishing a Merry Christmas and Happy New Year. Eventually, Prang and others began producing more conventional Christmas scenes.

In the early 1990s German publishers with even more accomplished methods of printing began producing dazzling postcards of Christmas greetings. Competing with Prang and others, they offered colorful illustrations of nativity scenes, evergreen trees, blazing fireplaces, and, of course, Santa Claus. For a time, Santa was portrayed in a purple outfit, brown robe, or green coat. Moreover, he was shown riding in an early automobile, talking on a curious device called the telephone, or even flying on an airborne dirigible. Most all of these assorted Santas are quite collectible today.

By the 1920s the so-called modern era of Christmas greeting cards was well underway, and glossy messages became a very important part of the seasonal celebration. Even during the Great Depression of the 1930s, cards were sold everywhere, from the mail-order Sears and Roebuck to Woolworth's vast department store chain. Greeting card sales rose from 30 million dollars per year in 1935 to an amazing 53 million dollars a year in the midst of war-torn 1943. Not only did cards dramatically change their approach from rather somber themes and verses, but they added patriotic, romantic, and even whimsical tones. The next 50 years saw an awesome variety of messages on Christmas greeting cards as well as those for every other major holiday. Since the 1970s well-wishers could also readily select greeting cards for any number of lesser holidays from Arbor Day to Saint Patrick's Day, not unlike the previous development of holiday postcards.

Shortly before Christmas in 1993, Hallmark, the world's largest greeting card company, announced from their headquarters in Kansas City that they would discontinue red and green envelopes for greeting cards because they stymied automated mail sorting. Actually, the company had not made the dark-colored envelopes since before Valentine's Day of the same year, but this was to be the first Christmas in many years of mostly white envelopes. It was a stark change for Hallmark, which produced 70 percent of their Christmas greeting cards with dark green and dark red envelopes in 1990. However, the company finally agreed to the change at the insistence of the U.S. Postal Service, which maintained such colors would seriously delay delivery. As smaller companies followed suit, the once-popular colored envelopes and their accompanying cards are likely to be another collectible commodity.

There are certainly many other Christmas-related paper collectibles. Since their inception in the early 1940s, Little Golden Books produced dozens of titles with Yuletide themes, including several editions of *The Night Before Christmas* and *Trim the*

Christmas Tree, a Little Golden Activity Book. In partnership with Walt Disney, the book company published many similar titles, including *Donald Duck and the Christmas Carol, Donald Duck and Santa Claus,* and *Mickey Mouse Flies the Christmas Mail.* Moreover, Christmas catalogs with large sections of toys, like the kind issued by major mail-order companies, have gained considerably in collecting status. Typically, a 1966 Christmas catalog from F.A.O. Schwartz—with Steiff animals, battery toys, and Matchbox vehicles pictured on 144 pages—is currently valued at $75. A Sears Christmas catalog from 1957 with 100 pages of toys, such as Roy Rogers items, Popeye vinyl doll, Coca-Cola dispenser, and a color section of Fisher-Price toys, would list slightly higher—$100 or more. Similarly, the 1941 Christmas book from Montgomery Ward, with 50 pages of toys—including Gene Autry Western outfits, trains, Porky Pig windup, and Superman Picture Projector Pistol—would be $100 plus.

Valentine's Day

Historians tend to consider valentines the first paper-related holiday greetings. English author Samuel Pepys confirmed the practice of written paper valentines in his diary in 1667: "This morning came up to my wife's bedside was little Will Merce to be her valentine, and he brought her name written upon blue paper in gold letters, done by himself: very pretty: and we were both pleased with it."

The idea of extending valentine greetings was well accepted by American colonists who adopted it from the British. In the 1730s booklets were available in the colonies and in England to assist the writer in preparing the proper message or verse. By the 1750s those with romance in their hearts could also find standard-sized, gilt-edged letter paper in the marketplace. This fine paper could then be painted, pin-pricked, cut out, and folded after the prepared message had been written in. Possibly the most finely detailed valentines arrived at the start of the 19th century when Germany immigrants brought with them the art of cutting paper valentines with scissors. Known as *scherenschnitte,* the craft has remained popular in parts of Pennsylvania for nearly 100 years. Such precisely cut valentines are considered folk art today and are displayed in many parts of the country.

Both kindly and dastardly cards did well with the Victorian public in England and the U.S. toward the turn of the century. Color and lace decorations were popular, as were mechanicals, valentine postcards, Kate Greenaway characters, Kewpies, and designs by specific artists. By the 1920s, as with many other holiday greetings in the U.S., folded valentines in envelopes were the trend. During the 1930s, 1940s, and 1950s, packages of valentines were widely exchanged among school children throughout the country. Additionally, full-sheet comic valentines, with an exaggerated character making anything from amusing to biting comments about the receiver, were popular with adults for more than half a century.

New Year's greeting postcard, 1909.

Thanksgiving

Thanksgiving is a uniquely American holiday. Little of it appeared on paper until the postcard zenith of the early 20th century. Thanksgiving cards often featured Pilgrims and Indians, turkeys, and people at the dinner table. As with most holiday postcards, the most prized Thanksgiving examples are from 1908 to 1915 and feature the signatures of leading artists of the period. Also sought are those from notable publishers like Tuck, International Art Company of New York, and John Winsch.

During the first quarter of the 20th century, the Singer Sewing Machine Company issued trading cards with embossed fruit and leaves proclaiming "Happy Thanksgiving." During the 1930s and 1940s and beyond, small and large stores around the country offered Thanksgiving greeting cards, paper tablecloths, nut cups and other paper decorations suitable for the holiday—all of which are collectible today.

Easter

Easter evolved as a significant commercial event in the United States during the second half of the 19th century, and by the early 20th century not only decorated eggs but also Easter greeting postcards had grown to be quite popular. Publishers who had mastered the lithographic process produced Easter cards ranging from those with somber messages to others depicting gaily colorful rabbits and baby chicks. Easter postcards of animals wearing the clothing of humans are a hit with collectors. Also of interest among holiday paper collectibles are Easter cards with children and rabbits or children with chicks. In later years the typical folded Easter card, like those of Christmas, became fashionable. In 1937 the Sears catalog offered "attractive Easter folders made to sell for more than double the Sears low price. Fine art work in glowing Easter colors, ten for 29¢."

New Years

As fate would have it, holiday greeting postcards came along in the late 19th century at about the same time as Americans decided to celebrate the new year with a bang. Research suggests that event before the first Tournament of Roses parade on January 1, 1886, the vision of a diapered baby with a banner across its chest had been shared with Americans by German immigrants. It is not surprising that some of the very first New Year's Day cards were printed in Germany and bore the traditional symbol.

Generally, the more valuable new year cards date prior to World War I. Sometimes special categories are singled out for New Year's Day card collecting such as those featuring pigs—a symbol of good luck and goodwill in the early 1900s, as were clovers, swastikas, coins, and horseshoes. As a result, the symbols were readily adopted for greeting the new year. Another popular image on the early New Year's Day cards is mushrooms, typically shown with elves. The cards also depict calendars, clocks, cats, and even Santas saying "Happy New Year."

RECOMMENDED READING

Christmas Past by Robert Brenner, Schiffer Publishing Ltd.

Christmas Through the Decades by Robert Brenner, Schiffer Publishing Ltd.

Official Price Guide to Holiday Collectibles by Helaine Fendelman and Jeri Schwartz, House of Collectibles.

Tomart's Price Guide to Golden Book Collectibles by Rebeca Greason, Wallace-Homestead.

PRICE LISTINGS

Christmas

Advertising poster, "Buy Christmas Seals," 1924, 11 × 14, $35

Card, Louis Prang, 1880s, color, $16

Card, Mickey Mouse, 1930s, yellow and green illustrations, Mickey shoveling snow, 4 × 4.5, unfolds to 8 × 8, Hall Brothers, Inc, $75

Card, Yule scene, 1940s, 3.5 × 3, $1

Catalog, Montgomery Ward, 1941, 50 pages of toys, 180 pages total, 8 × 11, $120

Louis Prang Christmas card, 1880s.

Catalog, Montgomery Ward, 1950, 80 pages, $125

Catalog, *Sears Christmas Book,* 1957, 100 pages of toys, 418 pages total, 8 × 11, $100

Catalog, *F.A.O. Schwartz Children's World,* 1966 Christmas catalog, 144 pages, 8 × 11, $80

Christmas card, 1940s.

Greeting card, Santa on TV set, 1950s, full color, imprinted, $2

Greeting card, choir boy with book, color, 1960s, $1

Little Golden Book, *The Night Before Christmas,* 1972, 24th printing, hardcover, 6.5 × 8, $3

Menu, Mobile Army Surgical Hospital, Christmas dinner, Camp Atterbury, December 25, 1950, cardboard, four pages, 5.5 × 8.5, $5

Print, *Judge* magazine, ca. 1890, color cartoon of King Christmas (Santa), 13.5 × 19.5, $30

Record album, "Gene Autry Merry Christmas," cardboard box with four 45-rpm sleeves, 1950, Columbia, $35

Toy store premium book, Pinocchio's Christmas Party, softcover, 16 pages, 1939, Disney characters, Watt & Shand, Lancaster, Pennsylvania, 8 × 10, $55

White House Christmas card, Richard Nixon, foldout card with white embossed scene White House, with envelope, December 1969, $32

Christmas greeting card, choir boy with book, 1960s.

White House Christmas card, Ronald Reagan, color illustration, original envelope, unused, 1982, 6 × 8, $25

Christmas greeting card, Santa on early TV set, 1950.

Little Golden Book, The Night Before Christmas, *1972.*

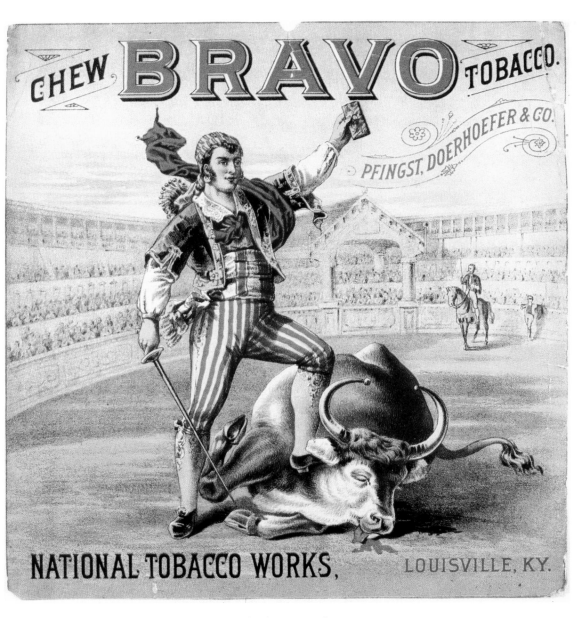

Bravo tobacco poster, 19th century.

Christmas card, ca. 1940s.

Greyhound racing program, 1946.

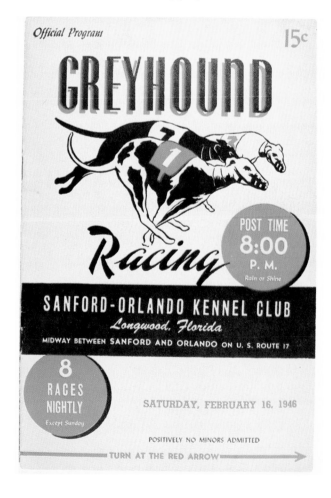

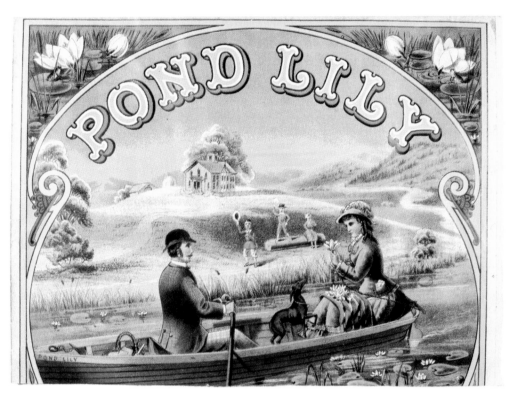

Pond Lily advertising label, 19th century.

TV World *magazine, 1953, Lucille Ball cover.*

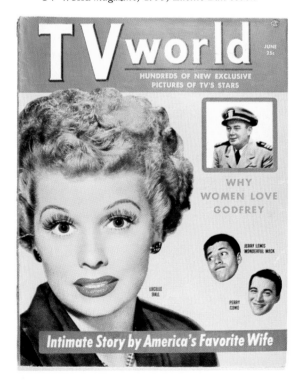

A-HEAD OF ALL OF THEM.

Trading card, Clark's O.N.T. thread, 19th century.

Time *magazine, 1961, John Kennedy inauguration.*

World Championship Rodeo program, 1935, Indianapolis, Indiana.

Political campaign handbook, 1940, published for The Pure Oil Co.

Advertising trade cards, late 19th century.

Tompkins Real Wild West show poster, 1910.

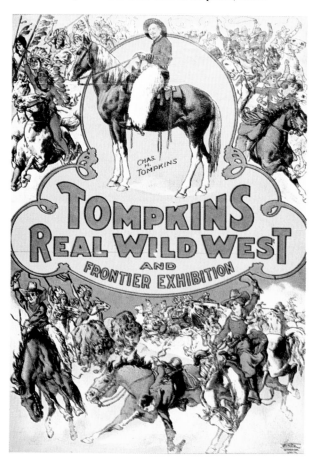

Coke advertising, 1961, National Geographic *magazine.*

Sports Illustrated *magazine, 1981, Tom Seaver cover.*

Liquor label, ca. 1930s, Old Black Joe brand.

Menu, Christmas dinner, Mobil Army Surgical Hospital (M.A.S.H.), 1950.

Wrapping paper, ca. 1938, department-store-sized roll, 3.5 × 26, 25 pounds, several hundred yards, Disney characters, $400

Easter

Postcard, "Happy Easter," 1990s, Hallmark, 6 × 4, $1

Trade card, greeting, 1890s, Woolson Spice Company, 4 × 5, $3

Halloween

Booklet, Clifford's Halloween by Normal Birdwell, softcover, 1966, 48 pages, 8 × 6, $5

Postcard, red witch and black cat, full color, 1912, $2

Sheet music, "Trick or Treat For Halloween," 1948, witch and Donald Duck's three nephews, Disney art by Carl Barks, 9 × 12, $80

Booklet, Clifford's Halloween, *softcover, 1966.*

Easter greeting trade card, 1890s, Woolson Spice Co.

Halloween postcard, red witch.

Valentine's Day

Card, comic, soldier boy and machine gun, color, 1940s, 2 × 3, $2

Card, comic, single sheet, Irishman in color on white paper, 1950s, printed in U.S.A., 9 × 6, $4

Card, greeting, Donald Duck, thick brown paper with black, red, yellow, and blue illustrations, 1946, Hallmark, 5 × 6, unfolds to 19 × 23, $75

Card, greeting, to teacher, 1950s, red and pink, $1

Card, greeting, Walt Disney, "My Lovely Blue Fairy," mechanical, 1939, W.D.P. (Walt Disney Productions), made in U.S.A., 5 × 5, $65

Card, greeting, Victorian woman, full color, turn of the century, 4.5 × 6.5, $3

Cards, comic Superman, group of 12, 1950s, each 8 × 11, color, in brown envelope by Panoco, $35

Comic valentine, single sheet, Irishman in color, 1950s.

Comic valentine, 1940s.

Valentine greeting card to teacher, 1950s, red and pink.

Leap year postcard, 1916, artist C.V. Dwiggins (Dwig).

Victorian valentine, full color, turn of the century.

New Year's greeting trade card, 1890s, Woolson Spice Co.

Studio portrait of young girl in flag dress, salt print, 1860s. Photo courtesy of Swann Galleries, Inc.

Other

Fourth of July, magazine, *Buckeye Republican Club,* 1928, red, white, and blue cover, 16 pages, 8 × 10, $15

Fourth of July, studio portrait, young girl in flag dress with flags, 1860s, salt print tinted with water colors, wooden frame, $825

Leap Year, postcard, rider on horseback, 1916, C.V. Dwiggins (Dwig), artist signed, $12

New Year's, greeting card, 1946, script message signed by Bess Truman, 4 × 6, matching franked envelope, $60

New Year's greeting trade card, 1900s, Woolson Spice Co., 4 × 5.5, $2

HOUSEHOLD ITEMS

Imagine test-driving the latest time machine for a little spin around the block back to the late 1950s. Instead of the *Twilight Zone,* enter a typical household with a treasure trove of paper collectibles. You would probably find a house filled with resourceful paper items not just from the 1950s period but also stocked—as households tend to be even today—with things dating from the prior 40 or 50 years. In reality, the whole first half of the 20th century sits on the counters, desks, ta-

TV Guide, Father Knows Best, *1956. Photo courtesy of Hake's Americana & Collectibles.*

bles, or in the drawers, closets, and garage of this place. Cooking pamphlets, newspapers, magazines, postcards, lots of reminders of World War II, and even early *TV Guides* would abound.

In the early 1980s while serving as editor of *Antique Week,* I received a telephone call from a writer/antiques dealer who often shared information. This time, my source was clearly saying *TV Guides* were hot items. Acquire some now, suggested the tipster, and have a solid investment ten years from now. At the time I had trouble with the idea of investing in paper collectibles in general and picking common old *TV Guides* in particular. I should have listened to the advice, of course. Such things are highly collectible today.

There was a time not so long ago when the experts were saying that magazines, for example, had no value and never would have any value. They were simply mass produced in such vast quantities that the supply would always exceed the demand. Try telling that today to the person who has a 1939 *Life* magazine with Joe DiMaggio on the cover, or a *TV Guide* with Elvis, or a *Saturday Evening Post* cover of President Eisenhower drawn by Norman Rockwell.

Meanwhile, for all their history, appreciation of newspapers from a collector's standpoint has only really grown in the last decade. Much of the credit has to go to sports memorabilia fans who discovered that old newspapers also gave space to sports. Right now, and in the foreseeable future, newspapers which document the feats of sports heroes will lead most any list of collectible newspapers—especially those from the 20th century. Of course, personalities in the news—good and bad—have strong appeal, as do major news events. The bigger, bolder, and splashier the headlines, the better.

Postcards certainly have been enduring, yet they still remain one of the most specialized of collectibles. Some collectors prefer distinguished artists of the past, such as Frances Brundage or Ellen Clapsaddle. Others prefer a particular topic, like airplanes or Boy Scouts, and still others go for holiday postcards—a specialty in which the more obscure holidays are usually the most highly prized. There is also a strong following for "real photo" cards, which were actually photographically processed—a more costly method than commercial printing.

Collectors are of course interested in a lot of other things around the house. Old catalogs, calendars, greeting cards, playing cards, and even stock certificates may not be on everyone's list but there surely are people who do have an interest in them and realize that they have some value. Often items like catalogs and calendars are sought by specialty collectors interested in a particular field. Items relating to firearms, ammunition, and sporting goods are avidly sought by those who have an interest in these popular collecting areas.

RECOMMENDED READING

American Sporting Advertising, Vol. 1 and 2 by Bob and Beverly Strauss, L-W Books.

The Official Price Guide to Post Cards by Diane Allmen, House of Collectibles.

The Official Price Guide to Paperbacks and Magazines by Charles and Donna Jordan, House of Collectibles.

Price Guide to Cookbooks and Recipe Leaflets by Linda Dickinson, Collector Books.

PRICE LISTINGS

Almanacs

Dr. Jayne's Medical Almanac, 1881, 5 × 7, $6

Swamp Root Almanac, 1925, $4.50

Shaker almanac, A.J. White, *How the Shakers Cook,* 1889, $40.

Catalogs

Premo Camera, catalog of (NY) Rochester Optical Co., 64 pages, 1896, $44

Sears, Spring & Summer catalog, 1937, 820 pages, $45

Dr. Jayne's Medical Almanac, *1881.*

Catalog, William M. Donaldson & Co., 1885, Cincinnati, Ohio.

Franklin D. Roosevelt on 1960 auto dealership calendar.

Cookbook and home canning guide, Ball Brothers Co., 1969.

Gardening catalog, embossed gilt cover, Peter Henderson Co., 160 pages, 1895, $12

Art supplies catalog, William Donaldson and Company, 24 pages, 1885, black-and-white photos, 10.5 × 8, $18

Calendars

Auto dealership, featuring Franklin Roosevelt, 1960, black and white, 24 × 36, $20

Mayo & Brothers Tobacco, 1881, $38

Pepsi-Cola, 12 sheets, 16 × 21, 1945, $45

Marlin Fire Arms Co., 3 × 6, 1904, $150

Franklin Pure Milk Co., 12 sheets, 1942, $11

Cookbook Pamphlets and Leaflets

Ball Brothers Co., cookbook and home canning guide, full-color cover, 1969, 100 pages, 6 × 9, $8

Complete Jello Recipes, color, 1929, $10

7-Up Goes To A Party, 15 pages, 1961, $5

Cooking Way Down South in Dixie, 1949, $12.50

Betty Crocker's Bisquick Cookbook, 1956, $4

A Cook's Tour with Minute Tapioca, 1931, $12

Greeting Cards

Original watercolor Christmas card, artist Adeline Gene, gold and pastel tones, 1909, $25

World War II special Christmas issue card, French Forces of the Interior, 1944, $25

Movable valentine in shape of a car, 1920s, $5

Thanksgiving greeting card with turkey, 1930s, $6–$8

Halloween children's party invitation, pumpkin and witch, 1940s, $3–$4

Magazines

American Legion, WWII articles and advertising, April 1945, pilot on full-color cover, 52 pages, $6

Women's Home Companion, spring fashions, April 1939, $8–$10

Life, Marilyn Monroe cover, April 7, 1952, $30–$35

Life, Kennedy assassination cover, November 1963, $20–$22

TV Guide, Jack Webb cover, April 10, 1953, $60–$65

TV Guide, Father Knows Best cover, June 16, 1956, $30

TV Guide, Elvis Presley cover, September 8, 1956, $85–$95

TV Guide, Beverly Hillbillies cover, March 9, 1963, $20

Saturday Evening Post, Eisenhower cover by Norman Rockwell, October 13, 1956, $18–$22

True Detective, Starkweather case, May 1958, $11–$14

TV Guide, Beverly Hillbillies, *1963. Photo courtesy of Hake's Americana & Collectibles.*

Newspapers

San Jose Mercury, Ruth hits two homers, June 6, 1926, $85–$90

Sacramento Bee, Moon landing, July 25, 1969, $8–$10

Philadelphia Evening Bulletin, Fall of Bataan, April 9, 1942, $8–$12

American Legion *magazine with pilot, 1945.*

Newspaper, 1927 Columbus Evening Dispatch *on Lindbergh.*

Bloomington Telephone (Ind.), Dillinger bank holdup suspect, May 18, 1934, $35

Columbus Dispatch (Ohio), Lindbergh reaches Nova Scotia, 1927, $30

San Francisco Chronicle, Nixon resigns, August 9, 1974, $12–$18

Playing Cards

Souvenir of Pittsburg, May Drug Co., 1905, $24

Pabst Blue Ribbon Beer, Baldwin Dist. Co., 1960, $5

Playing cards, late 19th century.

World War II postcard, black and white.

Old West '45, late 19th century, deck of 53, black and white, $35

Postcards

Valentine's Day with children, artist Ellen Clapsaddle, $3–$5

Trucking army style, World War II sketch, $2

Advertising, Singer Sewing Machine, early 20th century, $5–$8

Real photo, tourist bus, ca. 1920s, $5

Groundhog greetings from Punxsutawney, Pennsylvania, 1940s, $18–$20

Stock Certificates

Cincinnati, New Orleans & Texas Pacific Railroad, gray and white, 1920s, $15

The American Tobacco Co., Indian, orange, 1964, $10

World War II

Stationary, U.S. Army Air Force, engraved, 12-sheet package, $12–$15

Air Safety poster for pilot training, "Taxi Carefully," bright colors, 22 × 17, $20–$22

War Ration Book One with stamps, Office of Price Administration, $12

Booklet, *Pocket Reference Guide to Army, Navy, Marine Corps Insignia,* $8–$10

Hires Root Beer bottle topper, 1950s trading card offer.

Miscellaneous

Bottle topper, Hires Root Beer, full color, 1950s trading card offer, 7 × 6, $2

Greyhound bus schedule, 1949.

Bus schedule, 1949, Pennsylvania Greyhound, black and white, 3 × 4.5, unfolds to 9 × 12, excellent condition, $5

Cablegram, 1915, Great North Western Co., concerning Canadian victim of torpedoed *Lusitania,* $825

Customer booklet, Capitol Records, 1948, Margaret Whiting cover, 16 pages, articles and advertisements, black and white, 6 × 9, $5

Membership certificate, International Lions Club, 1945, orange and blue, 8 × 10, $8

Road map, Pure Oil Company, 1940s, Arkansas-Louisiana-Mississippi, blue and red, 5 × 9, $10

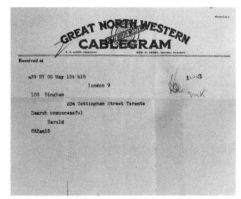

Cablegram relating to an unsuccessful Lusitania search, 1915. Photo courtesy of Swann Galleries, Inc.

Pure Oil trip map, 1940s, Arkansas, Louisiana, Mississippi.

Seed packet, Dodson Seed Store, Danville, Illinois, 1940s.

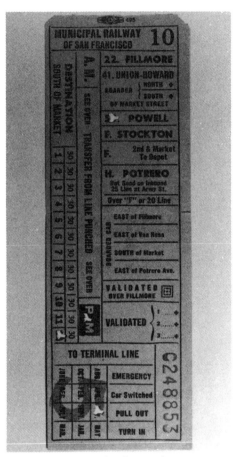

San Francisco municipal railway ticket, 1940s.

Seed packet, full color, 1940s, 3 × 4.5, Danville, Illinois, $2

Street map, St. Louis, Missouri, 21 × 27, Rand McNally, 1898, $18

Tourist pamphlet, Pikes Peak, Colorado Springs, Colorado, 1930s, red cover, black-and-white photos, 8 pages, 7.5 × 9, $8

Transportation ticket, Municipal Railway of San Francisco, 1940s, cream-colored paper, 2 × 6, $3

Travel brochure, Colorado Petrified Forest, black and white, 1930s, 3.5 × 6, $3

Travel brochure, S.S. *Catalina,* Santa Catalina Island, 1955, multiple colors, 4 × 9, $5

Brochure, *Boy Scout Uniforms & Accessories,* ca. 1940, $10

Pikes Peak travel brochure, Colorado Springs, Colorado, 1930s.

Petrified Forest travel folder, Colorado, 1930s.

Travel brochure, S.S. Catalina, *California, 1955.*

OFFICIAL DOCUMENTS

During the late 1980s a collector was interviewed about a full box of old documents she had discovered while administrating an estate. She described her feelings upon finding the box as similar to those of a child stumbling onto a whole chest of toys. The box holding the documents was itself a nice representative of 19th-century fold art. Rectangular in shape and painted over many times, it still bore the paneled sliding lid and thumb-grasp cut out at the lower center.

Few price guides devote much space to old documents in particular, but many can be found in specialty categories such as Civil War, 19th-century advertising, Western memorabilia, mining records, and similar groupings. Demand for routine documents of the 19th century and earlier is relatively low,

but that will surely change as we enter the 21st century and the electronic age. In 1994 one the country's leading newspapers reported that stock certificates issued in the 1970s by Ringling Brothers, Barnum & Bailey were worth about $500 each in mint condition. Part of the reason was the fact that they were decorated with clowns, animals, and trapeze artists—appealing subjects to those interested in circus-related collectibles. But another major factor, pointed out by the newspaper, is that even old stock certificates, especially those with ornamental designs, pictures, and other artwork, are becoming more collectible and valuable as electronic stock registration replaces them.

To some collectors the region identified in the document is of major importance. In-

Department of the Interior official business postcard, 1910.

dustrial areas, of course, produced more assorted documents than rural areas, and some parts of the country had an obvious headstart.

Land Grants

Official business documents, by their very nature, may overlap with other areas of paper collectibles. Yet, they were far more important in their time than most any other paper collectible.

In many ways, land grants are the quintessential form of official business paper, containing the essence of the official, legally binding type of document that has existed for centuries. A few years ago, a reader wrote a leading Midwestern newspaper asking for "complete anonymity" because she felt her land grants were so valuable, she would be robbed if somehow her identity became known. In response, the newspaper quoted an established dealer who advised her that United States land grants had been issued in such great numbers she should not worry too much about theft.

The answer was correct, more or less, but it left a great deal of the story untold. It also strongly (and wrongly) suggested to the reader that 19th-century land grants were

practically worthless. The revealing fact is that the vast majority of them, as attractive and striking as they are, were not actually signed by the president but by a secretary to the president. Still they are far from worthless—many land grants of this type typically sell for $30 to $40 each.

It is true land grants were issued in great numbers. Prior to 1833 these documents were printed on parchment and had to be signed by both the President and the Secretary of State or Land Commissioner. In the early days the government made a practice of giving a war veteran a land bonus in appreciation for service during wartime. Later they were issued for the purchase of public lands, mainly in Virginia and Ohio at first, but eventually in other states as well. Nearly 85,000 land grants had been issued for property in Ohio alone before 1833. They actually became a great drain on the president's time and when Congress finally passed a law in March of 1833 saying president Andrew Jackson could at last delegate the signing duty to a clerk and get on with the affairs of state, there was a backlog of over 20,000 such documents.

Therein, of course, rests the differences in the values of land grants. One issued in

1809, for example, with the authentic signatures of Thomas Jefferson and James Monroe would be worth well over $1,000. Those signed by either Monroe or Jackson alone would usually be worth several hundred dollars each. Generally, collectors who are serious about presidential signatures and are trying to complete a full collection think authentic signatures from early land grants are great.

Usually the "secretary signature" land grants of the late 1830s and the remainder of the 19th century appear on 10-by-16-inch sections of vellum paper with an ivory embossed seal at the bottom. However, there are many variations in these documents. Usually, the fine print on the majority of the secretary land grants carries the presidential name followed by with "by" and the secretary's name added under the name of the president. Those with bright, clear lettering and clean, fresh-looking paper are the most collectible.

Because of their significance in acquiring land, and because they were often one of the few official business documents a 19th-century family ever owned, they were frequently saved and passed from generation to generation. As a consequence, they can be found in fine condition in many parts of the country. Some collectors seek land grants from as many states as possible, or western states, or of as many 19th-century presidents as possible as represented by the secretary signatures.

Slavery

Official business documents dealing with slavery in America are often from the same period as the early land grants, but have an entirely different appeal—i.e., to collectors of African-American memorabilia. Some would view such material with disdain; however, it remains a very direct and authentic link to black history. During Black History Month in 1994, *USA Today* reported that slave documents had climbed considerably in value over the past 12 years, with some that once sold for $40 to $50 now bringing $450. The report also mentioned that some newspaper advertisements offering slaves were valued at $200.

While there may well be exceptions, careful collectors can still find a great deal of slave memorabilia in the $40 to $50 range. One company in North Carolina has offered 1840s and 1850s newspapers with slave ads from Kentucky, Virginia, and Louisiana at $10 to $12 per issue. (Vintage Cover Story, historical newspaper auctions, PO Box 975, Burlington, NC 27215. Catalog $6.)

Billheads and Letterheads

The westward movement was not fully underway until the 1850s, so billheads and other documents of the 1870s from Chicago and New York are readily available but comparable items from Dallas and Denver could be considerably harder to locate. Overall, attractive billheads and various legal documents from the nation's heartland, which feature manufacturers of that day, remain as interesting as governmental ones. Design and engraving are important as a part of the overall condition, especially to those with an eye for having the better ones framed. The historical content, whether governmental or commercial, is not to be overlooked, either. Most 19th-century documents, as has been mentioned, currently have relatively modest

Billhead with RCA logo, Stewart Talking Machine Co., 1919.

value. But nice examples are available, and there is also the possibility of finding a document or receipt signed by a once obscure clerk or landowner who went on to become a famous American. Or it might bear the signature of an historic personage who was merely signing what was an obscure document at the time.

Bills have been around for centuries, but only in recent years have they developed a significant following as a true collectible. Billheads were not that uncommon even during the American Revolution. However, they were rather plain affairs, generally showing only numbers and figures on what was otherwise a blank sheet of paper. Through the 19th century they developed a style of their own and proved to be the forerunner of the modern 20th-century letterhead. Increasingly from the middle to late 19th century, this business form included fine engravings of buildings, products, or various other illustrations. Particular companies and periods of time are now collectible as are regions of the country, as previously mentioned. Some collectors specialize in specific areas of commerce such as sporting goods, farm equipment, railroads, entertainment, or law enforcement.

During the first half of the 19th century, the livery stable or the tobacco warehouse occasionally added to their bills a black-and-white drawing of their place of business, but little more decoration was used. Eventually,

Letterhead and cover from Jeremiah Smith & Sons, Inc., Oyster Growers, 1920s. Photo courtesy of Hake's Americana & Collectibles.

printed sheets began to feature engraved pictures at the top. Embossed ornamentation was sometimes combined with the engravings, and printed billheads became common. Suddenly it was good business to promote your shop, factory, or office across the front of your billings. Eventually the column rules of earlier billheads were dropped, while the size of the images grew. By the 1890s there were teams of horses, plows, workers unloading carts, and numerous other signs of bustling enterprise—all at the top with lots of white space below. Sometimes the letterhead scenes were real, and sometimes they were exaggerated; but they all seemed to proclaim a growing commerce and prosperity.

Still another big boost for billheads and letterheads was the typewriter, which quickly

Check, 1919, Bunte Brothers, Chicago, Illinois.

became essential in virtually every office in America. The two made a perfect combination. During the 1920s and 1930s, leading companies tended to employ graphic designers instead of allowing the commercial engraver free reign. The result was that the ornate Victorian style gradually gave way to Art Deco and other styles. By the 1950s letterheads had become more restrained and, in most cases, unnecessary graphics were avoided.

Most of this paper material is fairly affordable. One exception is Shaker items which date from the 1860s to the 1880s and come from places such as Sabbathday Lake, Maine, and Mount Lebanon, New York. They can range in price from $50 on up to $200 or more. In recent years, a high price was paid for a bill endorsed by Christopher "Kit" Carson himself. It brought more than $500 at a national auction, while a petition to suspend a court-martial that was signed by Abraham Lincoln fetched over $1,000. Sold today, both would likely significantly surpass the previous prices. However, billheads, military orders, promissory notes, receipts, business letters, and governmental notices from the 19th century are usually found in the $10 to $30 range. As expected, some special seals, stamps, or markings can make them worth more.

Here are some tips to keep in mind in connection with collecting official business papers:

■ Antiques shops and malls are still a good place for discoveries. Specialized dealers may help with more specific types of paper wants.

■ Important and historical companies, like Wells Fargo or American Telephone and Telegraph command higher values, as do papers from important locations, like the Governor's Mansion in New York or the White House. Collectors could be competing with autograph hunters if the material includes signatures of important figures.

■ Generally, billheads and letterheads which have actually been used in business operations hold more collector interest than unused, blank sheets.

■ As companies go out of business or merge with others, great quantities of prior

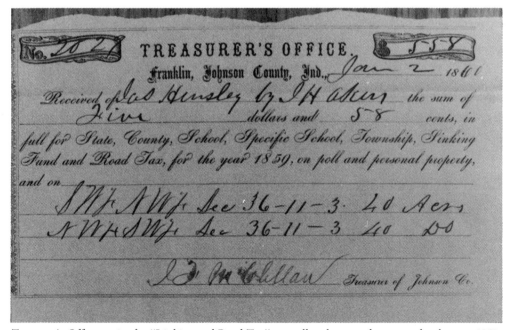

Treasurer's Office receipt for "Linking and Road Tax" on poll and personal property for the year 1859.

correspondence sometimes exists. Estates, likewise, sometimes contain company letters that have been saved for generations.

Again, this is a relatively young area of collecting with a future that appears very bright.

Old West Memorabilia

Of all the types of official business paper, the Old West is probably the most highly regarded today by collectors. Both government-issued and privately printed maps of the region attract collectors. Examples include the Santa Fe Railroad system from the 1880s, 1850s maps of California along with the "new" territories of Oregon, Washington, Utah, and New Mexico by Thomas, Cowperthwait & Company, or anything printed about Colorado in the 1880s.

In recent years a leading dealer on the East Coast offered a document signed by outlaw John Wesley Harding acknowledging his indebtedness in 1895 in Texas for 80¢ worth of rye whiskey and $3 lost playing dice. The price of the prized document of the Old West was $4,500. Mining stock certificates from Oregon and Colorado territories of the 1860s, with their colorful and well-illustrated scenes of work and industry in the western regions, are typically worth $60 to $80 today.

World War II

One of the most numerous official booklets of the century for American citizens rolled off the presses in March of 1942. Initially, there 190,000 copies of *War Ration Book No. 1* during the early days of World War II. At first, the books aimed to control quantities of sugar used, next came rationing of shoes, coffee, meat, and gasoline. More than half a century later, the carefully inscribed individual booklets or ration stamps—some in personalized leather pouches—are collectibles of the home front.

In fact, much of the material aimed at controlling the wartime marketplace, issued in great numbers by the Office of Price Administration and Civilian Supply and the War Production Board, is now sought out and collected. These two government agencies, along with many other official sources, also issued a vast array of posters designed to inspire Americans to help individually with the war effort. There are two basic groups of war posters—those that dealt with the war itself and those concerned with the home front. Women were a prime target of the posters on both fronts. Many were aimed at specific groups, such as nurses, factory workers, or the Women's Air Corps. Typically, the collector can expect to pay somewhat more

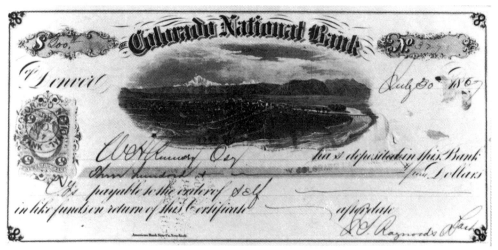

Bank draft from Colorado Territory, 1867, American Bank Note Co. Photo courtesy of American West Archives.

for the "blood and guts" posters of the war front than for those urging action back at home. However, those 1940s posters with female subjects have appreciated greatly in recent years and may eventually be the most highly regarded of the official government printings.

The posters ranged from one with a farm boy and a hayfork saying "Crop Troops Are Shock Troops" to a security-minded message warming "Keep The Enemy In the Dark." Some government posters simply said "Buy War Bonds" and these were common in the 1940s and are fairly available today. Homefront posters by artist N.C. Wyeth can be worth $500, and those by Norman Rockwell can also sell in the higher ranges. However, unknown and unsung artists created many of the posters for the government, along with artists like Hewitt, Ludekens, McCale, Packer, Norton, Woodburn, and Schlaikjer, and these are fairly affordable.

In late 1942, just a year after Pearl Harbor, *Life* magazine published a group of World War II posters, which were later credited to artists "armed with paint brushes, canvas, paper, and terrific determination to arouse the nation to winning the fight." Those posters were the last of their kind, and just 30 years later some of the same posters were being displayed in museums all over the nation, including the New York Museum of Modern Art. Despite the fact that many of these famed posters were routinely discarded in the years that followed the war, a number have survived in fairly good condition, and they continue to attract modern day collectors.

RECOMMENDED READING

Designing with Collectibles by Candace O. Manroe, Simon & Schuster.

Letterheads, 100 Years of Great Design by Leslie Cabarga, Chronicle Books.

Owning Western History by Warren Anderson, Mountain Press Publishing Company.

World War II Collectibles by Harry Rinker Jr. and Robert Heistand, Courage Books.

Pen, Ink, and Evidence by Joe Nickell, University Press of Kentucky.

Antique Maps, Sea Charts, City Views, Celestial Charts and Battle Plans by David Jolly, Jolly Publisher.

PRICE LISTINGS

Alien poll tax receipt, 1921, State of California, city of San Francisco, $10 annual tax, 3 × 6, $17.50

Authorization of a warrant to pardon John Connolly, May 22, 1874, signed by U.S. Grant, $500

Bill of sale, slave, 1847, state of Missouri, for sum of $100, "certain Negro boy named Abram, about 14, a slave for life," 6 × 7, $100

Book, *Keeping Faith, Memoirs of a President,* signed by Jimmy Carter, 1982, matching slipcase, 622 pages, $75

Boxed stationary, Women's Army Corps, 1940s, 50 each letterheads and envelopes, original box, $50

Civil War general orders, Washington, 1863, signed in type by E.D. Townsend, reporting on court-martial near Ft. Albany, Virginia, in which officer was convicted of absence without leave, 2 pages, very fine condition, $10

Confederate military telegram, March 12, 1862, General L.P. Walker at Huntsville to General Ruggles at Corinth, need for ammunition, $75

Credentials, U.S. Army Air Corps, folder and photos, worker Middleton Air Depot (Pennsylvania), ID card, etc. 1942, $85

Deposit slip for Bullion and Exchange Bank, 1888, Carson City, Nevada, used and initialed, 3 × 7, $3.50

Fire insurance policy, Franklin Fire, 1823, insuring Thomas Gibbons, three pages, 16 × 10, very fine condition, $65

Indian document, Cherokee Nation, chief T.M. Buffington, to pay for services of laundresses at the Insane Asylum, March 7, 1902, Tahlequah, Indian Territory, 12 × 8, $60

Land grant signed by governor of Pennsylvania, 1806, Gov. Thomas McKean, a singer of the Declaration of Independence, embossed seal, 12 × 21, very fine condition, $225

Land grants, six, 1839 to 1883, secretarial signatures of Fillmore, Polk, Buchanan, Arthur, Tyler, and Van Buren, five with nice seals, $200

Land grants, five, 1840s to 1880s, secretarial signatures of Grant, Pierce, Arthur, Tyler, and Van Buren, $175

Letter from astronaut Neil Armstrong to West Point General Willard Scott, declining invitation to graduation ceremonies, July 20, 1989, $225

Military letter, 1838, to Fort Dade, Florida, from commissary general, Washington, D.C., advising "sour crout" cost per barrel, during Seminole War, signed, $40

Payment document for slave, 1856, of W.A. Fishback, "$1,050 in full for one Negro slave named Anderson," 6 × 7, $75

Publication, *U.S. Navy in Vietnam,* 1968, Saigon publication, photos, 40 pages, $17.50

Printed statement of supplies, 1878, signed by Lt. Col. Elmer Otis, 7th Calvary, at Fort Rice, Dakota Territory, successor to General George Custer, $60

Presidential message card, printed note to troops from President Harry Truman, victory of American forces in Italy, signed by Gen. Mark Clark, with map, two pieces, 11 × 8.5, $85

Receipt, company, Adams Express from Sharps Rifle Company, $1 for box from New York to Bridgeport, 1876, $40

Receipt, government, for the sale of opium, 1940s, U.S. Treasury Department, 8 × 11, $12

Receipt, office, Chinese & Japanese Employment Office, for transportation to workplace $5, 1920s, San Francisco agency, 6 × 3.5, $22.50

Signature card, 1970s, Vice President Nelson Rockefeller, with seal and with assistant's note on vice-presidential letterhead regarding the signature, $30

Stock market document, with stock transfer stamps, 1925, Wall Street brokerage house, 4 × 7, $5

Typed letter, White House letterhead, signed Dwight Eisenhower, September 25, 1954, thanks to hotel executive, $200

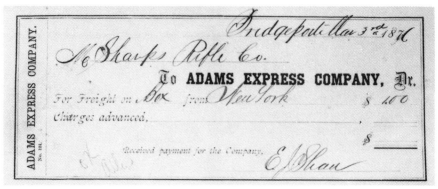

Adams Express Co. receipt from Sharps Rifle Co. for $1, March 3, 1876. Photo courtesy of Hake's Americana & Collectibles.

Wanted poster, 1934.

World War II poster.

Typed letter, White House letterhead, signed Franklin Roosevelt, March 15, 1939, thanks for invitation to attend anniversary celebration, $225

Wanted poster, 1934, John Dillinger with photograph, issued by federal government, 8 × 8, $139

Wanted poster, 1975, Patty Hearst, Emily Harris, William Harris, U.S. Department of Justice, 14 × 9.5, $80

White House card, 1950s, signed Mamie Doud Eisenhower, excellent condition, $75

World War II data, bound volume of 300 communiques, 1941 to 1943, daily battle action, U.S. Navy, 188 pages, index, fine condition, $75

World War II enemy alien ID book, for German national, travel limitations, photo, $15

World War II poster, "Give 'em Both Barrels," 1941, U.S. Government Printing Office, 15 × 20, $210

World War II poster, "Someone Talked," art by Siebel, 1940s, issued by the federal government, 14 × 22, $150

World War II propaganda leaflet dropped by Allied forces on Germany, advising that rockets came too late to end the war, peace is urged, very fine condition, $50

World War II ration books, one for sugar, one for coffee, two books, $25

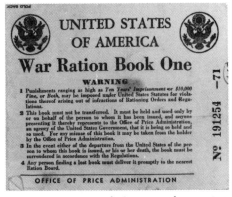

World War II Ratio Book One, *issued in 1942.*

PHOTOGRAPHS

There are really only two types of photographs for the collector to consider: those taken by the professional or even legendary photographer and those snapped by an amateur.

Professional

Professional photographs have long been valued and sought by the public. In fact, Swann Galleries in New York City has been auctioning fine examples since 1952. Highly prized are sports photographs from the 1930s by Ben Heller, images of Marilyn Monroe and other celebrities by Philippe Halsman, the 1950s works of Yousuf Karsh, and scenes from World War II by Constance Stuart Larrabee. Other desirable images include sports by Jim Dow, Native Americans by Fred Miller, personalities by Carl Van Vechten, urban scenes by Bernice Abbott, and also the photos of Margaret Bourke-White, Manual Alvarez Bravo, Edward S. Curtis, Edward Weston, and black photographers James Van Der Zee and Aaron Siskind.

A few years ago, a collector was browsing at a midwestern flea market when he came across an "interesting-looking old book." Upon closer examination he found that the illustrations were original photographs rather than reproductions. Recognizing the name of the photographer—Eadweard Muybridge from the 1870s—the collector made the purchase and began more extensive research. Eventually museum experts affirmed the rarity and historical significance of Muybridge's album of 121 photographs of the pacific coast of Central America and Mexico, taken between 1875 and 1877. Muybridge, who is better known for his later photographic studies of animals and people in motion, had been hired by the Pacific Mail Steamship Company to photograph sites of coffee cultivation and production in Mexico, Panama, and Guatemala in an attempt to lure American investment to the region. The negatives were destroyed by fire after only a few albums were assembled. Eight albums are in institutional libraries; each differs in the selection of images. No one know if more sets survived. Ultimately, the album of original photographs sold at auction for more than $57,000.

A collectible area akin to professional photographs are promotional photographs distributed singly or in press/media kits from major agencies involved in publicity. Sources range from leading corporations and institutions to television networks and public relations firms. Here the collectibility usually depends not on the photographer but on the topic or personality depicted.

Along similar lines are wire service photos from the 1930s through the 1960s, (usually eight by ten inches and glossy black and white) and movie stills, which were frequently issued in media kits or press books by major movie producers and are similar in

Cabinet card, ca. 1880, Wyatt and Morgan Earp with Doc Holliday. Photo courtesy of Swann Galleries, Inc.

format and design to wire service photos. Both gradually drifted into collector circles after original distribution to journalists and news organizations. Movie stills were also sometimes given to movie distributors and theater owners.

The old adage "You never know until you ask" is alive and well when it comes to collectible photographs. Chalmers M. Roberts wrote a delightful little book in 1991 about reaching 80 years of age. In a brief section of *How Did I Get Here So Fast,* he described tracking down some authentic Civil War photographs:

> *When visiting Washington, D.C., as a young man, he visited two elderly ladies who were the daughters of Levin Handy, an apprentice to famed Civil War photographer Mathew Brady. At the time the two were widowed and living in a small brick house in the nation's capital. They still possessed a number of original glass-plate negatives that had been passed down from their father, who had obtained them from Brady. The daughters sold Roberts the original prints from two of the negatives, including one of Abraham Lincoln which had served as the model for the five-dollar bill. The prints even bore the red stamp from L.C. Handy Studios starting "successor to Mathew Brady, the oldest commercial studios in the United States."*

Amateur

Amateur vintage photographs are another matter. Probably every home in America once had an accumulation of family photographs stashed somewhere. In the album or shoebox were scores of images ranging from rather obscure relatives to events of an inspired but undistinguished childhood.

Up until the middle 1950s, the average at-home photographer took everything in black and white with a Kodak camera or something similar. Until that time most color

work was limited to portraits done in professional studios, and often many of those were actually "retouched" by hand painting colors onto basic black-and-white photos. Like black-and-white movies, black-and-white pictures gathered dust in the family photograph albums while everyone's attention was captured by "living color" and its future prospects.

By the 1960s, although color prints were commonplace, basic family photography was beginning to wane. The standard photograph, in some cases, gave way to the brilliance of the color slide that could be projected onto a screen or wall. Moreover, many families could afford the primitive home movie cameras, which eventually progressed to the refinement of the home video camera. One result of all this technological advancement (not to mention the decline of the nuclear family and the tendency not to maintain photographs of unknown relatives) was the leaving behind of a treasure trove of black-and-white pictures. Today, from the turn-of-the-century peanut vendor with the stern look to the Great Flood of the Ohio River in 1937, they are quite collectible. First of all, they reflect a way of life that has long since disappeared. Just as importantly, the vintage photos are among the few remaining things that were created directly by the people involved in the daily living of America's past.

Like postcards—and more specifically real photo postcards—vintage photos undoubtedly lend themselves to topical categories such as stores and businesses, transportation, musical uniforms and instruments, sports, occupations, disasters, ethnic groups, and political events. There is also the potential for high collectibility within the various decades, the 1940s, 1950s, and 1960s. Approximate dates can be determined by the various scenes and events such as the appearance of the streets, neighborhoods, fashions, leisure activities, dolls and toys, and commercial districts.

Collections of old photographs can, of course, be found anywhere, from the closet to the antiques mall. However, while there are lots of turn-of-the-century professionally done portraits in shops, vintage photos of the early and middle 20th century are somewhat less available. The ultimate source for significant photographs would be the leading auction galleries such as Swanns. The serious collector can obtain one of Swann's photograph auction catalogs, issued semiannually, for about $25. The book, fully illustrated, includes 600-plus pages, estimated values, and index. Realized prices following the catalog's numbering system are also provided to the subscriber after the sale. Catalog orders can be sent to Swann Galleries, Inc. at 104 East 25th Street, New York, NY 10010, or by calling (212) 254-4710.

RECOMMENDED READING

Collector's Guide to Early Photographs by O. Henry Mace, Wallace-Homestead Company.

An Iowa Album: A Photographic History, 1860–1920 by Mary Bennett, University of Iowa Press.

Shadow and Substance: Essays on the History of Photography edited by Kathleen Collins, University of New Mexico Press.

PRICE LISTINGS

African-American

> Carte de visite, Blind Tom, ca. 1864, with tax revenue stamp on back, $165 (Swann Galleries)

Business

> Street-side peanut vendor, ca. 1918, $6

Storefront, 1880s, Baumgart & Axt.

> Storefront, print shop and two printers, 1942, real photo postcard, $6

> Storefront, store and two merchants, 1880s, $16

Disasters

> 1937 flood, 3.5 × 5.5, downtown Louisville, Kentucky, $12

> Tornado damage to small southern town, 3 × 5, 1920s, $5

Printing business, 1942, real photo postcard.

Picture of 1937 flood at Louisville, Kentucky.

Tornado strikes southern town, 1920s, black and white.

Wire service photo, actress Lucille Ball, 1963, Desilu Productions.

Entertainment

Tony Orlando and Charro, 1974, CBS television network publicity photograph, $5

Lucille Ball as president of Desilu Productions, 1963 wire service photo, black and white, $20

Our Gang at birthday party, glossy 8 × 10, mint condition, $5

Gunsmoke's *Jim Arness, 1966, wire service photo.*

Tony Orlando and Charro, CBS TV promotion photo, 1974, black and white.

James Arness in scene from *Gunsmoke,* 1966 wire service photo, black and white, $18

Monte Hale, 1948 movie still, *California Firebrand,* $12

Movie still, Republic Pictures, California
Firebrand *starring Monte Hale, 1948.*

Child with doll, 1940s, black and white.

Band member in uniform, 1953, black and white.

Family Portrait

Composite family photo, 1879, large
albumen print, photographer G.H.
Field, $192 (Swann Galleries)

Individuals

Astronaut Neil Armstrong on the moon,
1969, silver print, $1,100 (Swann
Galleries)

Cheyene Indian, ca. 1900, portrait
photo, silver print, $350

Little girl with doll, 1940s, snapshot, $3

Military

Military group in uniforms, 1890s,
courthouse background, $18

Civil War, 1865, Johnson's Mill,
Petersburg, Virginia, $165 (Swann
Galleries)

Musical

Teen girl in full band uniform with
trombone, 5 × 7, 1950s, $8

*Carte de visite of Jefferson Davis and his wife,
Varina Howell Davis, 1860s.*

Public Officials

Carte de viste of Jefferson Davis and wife Varina Howell Davis, 1860s, $475

Wire service photo, July 1963, John Kennedy and daughter Caroline, $21

Official media kit photo, 1960, John Kennedy and wife and daughter, $28

Real photo postcard, 1940s, Vice President and Mrs. John Garner, $6

Wire service photo, August 1963, Martin Luther King at Lincoln Memorial, $50

Wire service photo, 1969, Abbie Hoffman of the Chicago 7, $12

Sports

Cincinnati Redlegs player George Crow in uniform, 1950s, real photo postcard, $7

Abbie Hoffman of Chicago 7, antiwar rally, 1969, wire service photo.

Vice President John Garner and wife, real photo postcard, 1940.

Martin Luther King at Lincoln Memorial, 1963, wire service photo.

Indianapolis 500 Motor Speedway race, 1961, 5 × 7, black and white, $5

Hot-air balloon ascension, ca. 1910, $8

Wide World of Sports promotion photo, 1974, boxers Muhammad Ali and Joe Frazier, 8 × 10, black and white, $5

Men's team, basketball, 1929, $9

Transportation

Snapshot, two children and 1947 Chevrolet sedan, $3

Snapshot, two women with car, dated 1929, $4

Snapshot, boy with 1950s automobile, $2

Real photo postcard, 1940s truck stop, Marietta, Georgia, $10

News photo, Hidenburg in flight, 1930s, silver print by Underwood & Underwood for Universal Newsreel, $220 (Swann Galleries)

Weddings

Bride and groom with bridesmaid and best man, 1934, studio portrait, $6

Bride with seated groom, 1898, studio portrait, $5

Indianapolis Motor Speedway, 1961, black and white, 5 × 7.

Hot-air balloon ascension, ca. 1910.

Family sedan, Chevrolet, 1947, black and white, Kodak.

Wide World of Sports *promotion photo, 1974, Mohammed Ali and Joe Frazier.*

Parking lot, early 1950s, Indianapolis, Indiana, black and white.

Bride and groom wedding photograph, ca. 1898, full wedding attire.

Ladies of fashion, 1929, black-and-white snapshot.

Wedding party, 1934, Midwest.

POLITICAL

In 1980 John Connally made an appearance in a midwestern city for a promising Congressional candidate. Connally, who had ridden with Kennedy on that fateful day in 1963, had been elected governor of Texas, had served in the Johnson administration, and had done amazingly well in his own presidential campaign, asked of the candidate's manager: "How much of your campaign funds are you spending on television advertising?" "Well," replied the campaign manager, "about 50 percent of it." "If I were you," quipped Governor Connally dryly, "I'd up that to about 100 percent."

The very politically astute Connally made a point that would soon become a lasting tradition in America politics—every penny that can be poured into TV commercials, will be poured into TV commercials. The result, nationally, has been a dramatic drop in paper memorabilia produced in presidential campaigns since the late 1970s. Posters (except for yard signs), pamphlets, bumper stickers, window stickers, cards, and paper banners have all but disappeared on the campaign trail.

In 1968, officials of the Democratic National Convention decided that the hostile climate of the political times called for extreme security measures. One of those measures was electronically monitored credentials for delegates, journalists, and party officials. Inside the layers of rubberized cards were metal codes which could be read by machines as visitors entered the convention hall. The system didn't work perfectly, but it was effective enough to forever change the appearance and content of press passes, delegate credentials, and admission tickets. No longer would anything involving official admission to a national political convention be just plain paper.

Ironically, Americans seem to be growing more interested in collecting political memorabilia and less interested in participating in the process. According to the U.S. Department of Commerce, 63 percent of those surveyed in the 1950s said they had voted in the last presidential election and hardly anyone thought of collecting. In the 1990s, only 50 percent of those surveyed said they had voted in last presidential election, and collecting political material is at record levels. In the years ahead demand will significantly increase for the really nice presidential campaign material of the 20th century— pieces kept in fine condition that are a direct product of a once-in-four-years historical event. The golden era of such things will likely be seen as the 1960s, with TV and other demands gradually contributing to the near-total demise of political paper in a few generations.

Winners and Losers

Hake's Americana lists Abraham Lincoln, Theodore Roosevelt, Franklin Roosevelt, Harry Truman, and Richard Nixon, after John Kennedy, as presidents very popular with collectors. Additionally, collectors are challenged to find quality paper campaign memorabilia of some of the big presidential candidates who lost. Often those who were totally sacked in 20th century elections had spent far less money and their campaigns, therefore, produced considerably less material. Warren Harding grabbed nearly 64 percent of the vote in defeating James Cox in 1920. Franklin Roosevelt bested Alf Landon with 60 percent of the vote in 1936, as did Theodore Roosevelt over Alton Parker in 1904, Lyndon Johnson against Barry Goldwater in 1964, and Richard Nixon with George McGovern in 1972.

Magazines and Newspapers

With popular campaigners as well as with losers, newspapers and magazines are one of the best sources of political paper. Newspapers that scream the results and news magazines which have covers of presidential potentials can still be readily found in fine condition. Also colorful and collectible are the special presidential election issues published by *Time* and *Newsweek* every four years.

One of the most highly collectible of the paper political items in the country happens to be a newspaper—the classic *Chicago Tribune* from 1948 erroneously proclaiming "Dewey Defeats Truman." Adding to the story and the collectibility of the newspaper is the famous photograph of beaming presidential victor Harry Truman holding up the newspaper from his speaking podium. The newspaper now commands several hundred dollars. The silver print photograph taken by Frank Cancellare was auctioned at Swann Galleries in 1992. It had a presale estimate of $600 to $900 but eventually brought more than $1,500.

Kennedy Memorabilia

In the early 1960s practically every evening newspaper in America had a deadline no later than 1 p.m. This was the latest most single-edition dailies could wait for stories and still allow time for composing and printing and delivery by supper time. Up until that time, new services, like United Press International and Associated Press, provided a steady stream of national and international stories. Newsrooms everywhere were filled with the clatter of wire service teletypes as electronically activated keys hit wide and endless rolls of yellow paper and editors hurriedly scanned the material for last-minute use. After the busy afternoon news deadline, the wire services coasted with the day's stock market report and most editors began looking for a late lunch.

On one particular day, I had returned to the wire service machine as it routinely typed out the stock prices. I was hoping that somehow our native-son candidate would officially announce his intentions to run for governor of the state. Our hometown newspaper had basically already unofficially broken the story a few days earlier, but the official announcement would also be very big news in our community. The stock report droned on as it did every day. Lockheed was at 36, Monsanto at 54, and National Dairy at 64. The teletype stopped abruptly at Pacific Telephone. Suddenly the teletype's bell was clanking from within the machine. It was a simple device to alert news editors who may have been busy with other tasks that a major story was breaking or an older one was being significantly updated.

I seriously doubted that UPI would interrupt the stock report for my guy's gubernatorial announcement, but I was curious. "Preceding Kennedy," it typed, meaning there was a follow-up to the president's visit to Dallas, Texas. "BULLETIN," immediately followed that, then a frantic ringing of the alert bell. The few people in our newsroom began looking up.

The wire machine immediately typed "FLASH." This was a rare term at the time, seldom used by wire services. A typical news editor may not encounter such a message in years of desk duty. "Kennedy seriously wounded," the teletype clattered, then in capital letters, "PERHAPS FATALLY BY ASSASSIN'S BULLET."

Everyone living today who was alive then, of course, has their very own moving story of that tragic event. Mine began with the yellow teletype paper which I had so frantically ripped off the machine and which I have so carefully saved ever since. No collectibles market that I know of has yet offered any wire service teletype copy dealing with the death of President John Kennedy, or, for that matter, dealing with any of the events of the 1950s and 1960s. Of all the dramatic stories transmitted to daily newspapers around the country, very little of the actual paper was saved. When this type of material finally disappeared with the arrival of the electronic age, almost no one noticed it was gone.

Kennedy is a good focus for political memorabilia because, in most circles, he is considered the most collectible of all of America's presidents. To be sure, there are collectibles associated with every president of the United States, and some have considerable value, such as those related to George Washington or Abraham Lincoln. None, however, command the numbers of collectors that John Kennedy memorabilia does.

Kennedy served in the White House less than three years, which makes his the shortest term of any 20th-century president. When he was killed in November of 1963, there was a rush to save material related not only to the assassination itself but to his presidency. In the years that followed there were also a number of memorial items made of paper and other materials. All these things tend to leave the impression that Kennedy material would remain in abundant supply and not be in too much demand among later generations. However, after 30 years or so, collectors and dealers have realized that a lot of America's closets have been cleaned out since that shocking event.

Kennedy collectibles are frequently divided into three categories: the 1960 campaign, material generated during the relatively brief time he served in the White House, and memorial items, which were issued in the months and years immediately after his death. Material specifically from

JFK's single presidential campaign are highly sought, in part because of his popularity, but also because there is less of it than most observers—even collectors—might expect. The amount of money spent on Kennedy's campaign, despite the family's great wealth, was one of the smallest of any modern major party nominee. Most of it, especially paper material, was used and discarded as the photo-finish campaign ended.

Media kits issued by the Kennedy campaign were distributed to thousands of newspapers in 1960, but because of limited finances, they were rather sparsely made. Those given to weekly newspapers came in plain yellow folders and contained biographical sheets on both Kennedy and Lyndon Johnson. Also included in the kits were official black-and-white photographs of the Kennedy family. Campaign brochures were also somewhat limited. One of the most popular was a red, white, and blue "Time for Greatness" folder, which featured a number of black-and-white photos. There were also bumper stickers and shield-shaped window stickers, which were fairly few in number and destined by their very nature to be used during the campaign and then scraped off and thrown away.

Another source of JFK campaign material is the media itself. Newspapers provided massive election coverage, and Kennedy and his family also appeared in the leading magazines of the day. A demonstration on his behalf at the National Democratic Convention was featured on the cover of *Life* magazine in July of 1960. John and Jacqueline appeared together on the cover of *Life* in November of 1960. The inauguration of President Kennedy in January of 1961 was prominently featured in newspapers and magazines of the era. There were also several different types of inaugural souvenirs which featured the president, sometimes by himself and sometimes with Vice President Johnson. A souvenir inauguration invitation with black text and the gold embossed presidential seal brought $69 in the first Kennedy memorabilia auction held by Hake in 1993.

News service photographs of the Kennedy White House years have begun attracting significant attention. These glossy, black-and-white pictures, stamped with the names of the news organization on the back and bearing a few lines of news information on the front, have been featured at prestigious Swann Gallery auctions in New York, Hake's in Pennsylvania, and at other sales. They were sold in small groups at Swann's during the early 1990s for several hundred dollars per lot, although prices were considerably less at Hake's. A complete issue of the *New York Times* on the day Kennedy was killed lists at around $25. However, collectors attach more value to the daily newspaper issued in Dallas where the event actually occurred.

"More people collect the memorabilia associated with Kennedy than any other president," confirmed Ted Hake of Hake's leading collectibles and Americana marketplace in 1994. Hake based his opinion on over 25 years of monitoring the country's collecting interests, plus conducting more than 125 mail and phone auctions, which nearly always included political memorabilia.

John Kennedy's brother Bobby was involved in his own presidential campaign for only a few months before he was killed in California in 1968. Shortly before his assassination, Graphic Colorplate in Stamford, Connecticut, printed a very unflattering and abstract poster of the candidate to be used as a centerfold for *Cheetah* magazine. When the assassination occurred, the entire press run of the "Yellow Peril, 1968" poster was supposedly destroyed. However, the pressman on the job had taken one poster home the day before. In 1993 this only known surviving example—showing a brightly clothed RFK holding a blue dove in one hand and a samurai sword in the other—sold at auction for several hundred dollars.

In 1993, Hake held an auction devoted entirely to Kennedy material, including items from the campaigns of John, Bobby, and Ted. In all, more than 1,000 items were sold. "Such material reaches out well beyond the political collecting hobby to people in other fields," remarked Hake. "There is simply a very broad interest in Kennedy collectibles."

RECOMMENDED READING

The Official Price Guide to Political Memorabilia by Richard Friz, House of Collectibles.

Hake's Guide To Presidential Campaign Collectibles by Ted Hake, Wallace-Homestead.

PRICE LISTINGS

Advertising card, Grant and Tilden, 1870s, 3 × 5, $45

Business card, FDR law office announcement, 1925, 3.5 by 5.5, $135

Campaign booklet, William Jennings Bryan, 1908, 60 pages, $60

Campaign brochure, Richard Nixon, 1968, mock *Time* magazine cover, four pages, red and white border, 8 × 10, $14

Carte de visite of Lincoln, 1860s, approximately 2 × 3, $60

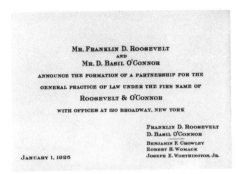

Card announcing FDR opening law office, dated January 1, 1925. Photo courtesy of Hake's Americana & Collectibles.

Centerfold poster, Robert Kennedy, 1968, *Cheetah* magazine, 10 × 24, $300

Cigarette package, "I Like Ike," 1952, taped cellophane, $70

Coloring book, John Kennedy, 1960s, 24 pages, black-and-white illustrations, $21

Grant-Tilden advertising card for Blackwell's Tobacco, 1870s. Photo courtesy of Hake's Americana & Collectibles.

Lincoln carte de visite, Lincoln, Mary, and their two sons, 1860s.

"I Like Ike" cigarettes, 1952. Photo courtesy of Hake's Americana & Collectibles.

RFK poster to be used as centerfold in Cheetah *magazine, 1968. After assassination occurred, the press run was destroyed. Photo courtesy of Hake's Americana & Collectibles.*

Dollar certificate, Dewey-Warren, 1948, green and black, approximately 3 × 7, $12

Election ballot, Grover Cleveland and Thomas Hendricks, 1884, 7 × 3, $55

Inaugural escort pass, Ronald Reagan, 1981, $4

Inaugural invitation, Jimmy Carter, 1977, mint, $9.50

Invitations and programs to inauguration of FDR (two), 1937, original envelopes, (Swann auction) $121

Magazine, *TV Guide,* 1956, week of Democratic National Convention, $15

Inaugural escort ticket, 1981, Ronald Reagan.

Vote for the
Candidates of
the Roosevelt
Democracy in
Pennsylvania

For United States Senator
JOSEPH F. GUFFEY ☒

For Governor
GEORGE H. EARLE ☒

For Lieutenant Governor
THOMAS KENNEDY ☒

For Secretary of Internal Affairs
THOMAS A. LOGUE ☒

For Superior Court Judge
CHESTER H. RHODES ☒

Primaries, Tuesday, May 15, 1934

*FDR poll card for primary election, 1934. Photo
courtesy of Hake's Americana & Collectibles.*

Magazine, *Time,* JFK inauguration cover
in color, January 27, 1961, $14

Membership card, Michigan Democratic
Party, 1963, official signatures, JFK
and FDR on front, approximately 2
× 3, $15

Menu, dinner, Teddy Roosevelt, 1902,
presidential seal, Cincinnati Fall
Festival Association, stiff paper sheet,
6 × 8, $35

New England States Are For Taft

*Taft postcard, 1907. Photo courtesy of Hake's
Americana & Collectibles.*

*Kennedy campaign poster, 1960. Photo courtesy of
Hake's Americana & Collectibles.*

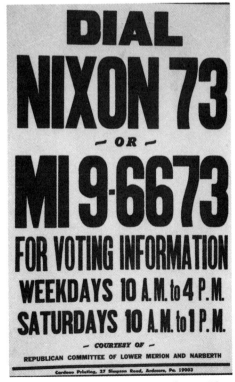

*Nixon campaign poster, 1972, Pennsylvania. Photo
courtesy of Hake's Americana & Collectibles.*

Newspaper, John Kennedy assassination, November 23, 1963, Washington Post, $18

Newspaper, Nixon Resigns, August 9, 1974, Washington Post, $22

Newspaper, campaign, *Re-Elector,* Committee for Re-Election of President Nixon, July 1972, $20

Newspaper, "Connecticut First for Kennedy," November 9, 1960, *New York Daily News,* $20

Pamphlet, campaign, *Kennedy for President,* 1960, red, white and blue, black-and-white photos, 3 × 8, $50

Poll card, Franklin Roosevelt, primary election, 1934, 2 × 4, $18

Postcard, William Howard Taft, 1907, black and white with popular vote, $40

Reagan-Bush campaign poster, 1984. Photo courtesy of Hake's Americana & Collectibles.

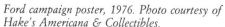

Ford campaign poster, 1976. Photo courtesy of Hake's Americana & Collectibles.

Mondale campaign poster, 1984. Photo courtesy of Hake's Americana & Collectibles.

Poster, campaign, John Kennedy, 1960, red, white and blue, 13 × 20, $55

Poster, campaign, Richard Nixon in Pennsylvania, 1972, 14 × 22, $25

Poster, campaign, Gerald Ford, 1976, full-color photo, 15 × 25, $18

Poster, campaign, Reagan-Bush jugate, 1980, $25

Poster, campaign, Walter Mondale, 1984, National Education Association, 14 × 20, $12

Poster, campaign, Robert Kennedy, 1968, red and blue, 24 × 38, $65

Program, FDR inauguration day, March 4, 1933, 8 pages, $60

Sheet music, John Kennedy, 1960, "Kennedy Victory Song" by Fleiz A. Nolasco, four pages, 9 × 12, $45

Ticket, admission, Democratic National Convention, July 1992, with holograph, original envelope, $6.50

Ticket, admission, Republican National Convention, 1912, McKinley on front, $20

Ticket, convention, National Progressive Party, 1912, Lincoln, Jefferson, Washington on front, $64

Ticket, guest, Democratic National Convention, 1920, Wilson on front, $20

Ticket, guest, Democratic National Convention, 1924, New York, 3 × 5, $25

Convention ticket, 1912, Chicago. Photo courtesy of Hake's Americana & Collectibles.

Democratic National Convention guest ticket with Woodrow Wilson on front, 1920, San Francisco. Photo courtesy of Hake's Americana & Collectibles.

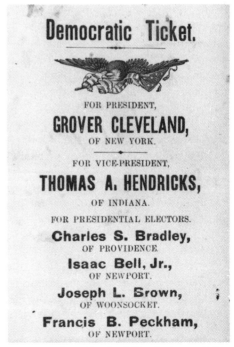

Democratic ticket, Cleveland-Hendricks, ca. 1884. Photo courtesy of Hake's Americana & Collectibles.

Republican Convention guest ticket, 1912, with McKinley on front. Photo courtesy of Hake's Americana & Collectibles.

Ticket, party, Democratic, 1884,
Cleveland and Hendricks, white
paper, approximately 3 × 5, $44

Ticket, reception, Vice President
Agnew's inaugural, 1973, 7 × 4, $5

Window sticker, Kennedy for President,
1960, shield design, die cut, red,
white, blue, 6 × 8, $35

POPULAR CULTURE
School Days Memorabilia

In my opinion, the two true icons of
American culture in this century were not
Lucy and Desi, Tom and Jerry, Reagan and
Bush, or Masters and Johnson, but Dick and
Jane. Growing up with this amazing fictional
family in elementary school left a lasting impact. My little black-and-white dog was
named just like the one in all the reading class
materials—not just "Spot," "See Spot."

From the 1930s through much of the
1960s, millions of youngsters learned to read
by way of the life and times of Dick and Jane.
Many of today's adults remember them and
the rest of their family, including Bill Clinton
who, during the 1992 presidential campaign
fondly reminisced about his grandparents
reading the Dick and Jane books to him.
Reportedly, he still has one of the old readers
in his personal library.

In the series, Father always wore a suit,
drove the car, and went off to work, while
Mother donned an apron and high heels and
stayed in the kitchen. Jane helped Mother
with the chores, while Dick sailed paper airplanes. The books eventually went out of
print after criticism that the white, middle-
class family lacked ethnic diversity and per-
petuated gender stereotypes. In 1965 the
publisher had added a multi-ethnic edition,
which featured a black family that moved into
the Dick-and-Jane neighborhood, but this re-
vision was too little too late. Even in the early
years Dick and Jane represented a very idealized family that never existed in real life.
Their most important contribution, however,

was not their lifestyle but the fact that they
taught millions the joy of reading.

For a time in the 1980s, collectors could
find the classic Dick and Jane reading text-
books for $30 to $60, but in recent years they
have all but disappeared. In 1994, two major
exhibits of Dick and Jane memorabilia were
held in this country, one at the Public Library
in Richmond, Virginia, and another at the
Lakeview Museum of Arts and Sciences in
Peoria, Illinois. In connection with the
events, Associated Press talked with James D.
Keeline, manager of Prince and the Pauper
Collectible Children's Books in San Diego,
California. Keeline said the materials were
produced in the millions but only a fraction
survive today. As a result, originals sell for
$75 to $300, according to Keeline, depending
on condition and how prominent a role Dick
and Jane themselves play in the stories.

A few years ago we were commissioned
by a national magazine to do an article on
Dick and Jane collectibles. The materials
were to be shipped to the magazine's office to
be photographed with special equipment.
The problem was we just could not come up
with enough good material to properly illus-
trate the article. Scott, Foresman and Company keeps an almost-complete set of approximately 100 different Dick and Jane
readers, workbooks, and teacher's guides in
their headquarters at Glenview, New York,
You can look at them there, you just can't
check them out anymore.

Actually, a great number of the things of
elementary school are rapidly rising in status
in the paper collectibles world. The thank-
you notes, listings of the day's lunch, School
Safety Patrol membership cards, *Weekly
Readers,* workbooks, notebooks, printed copies of the Pledge of Allegiance, class pictures,
test papers, and even grade-school report
cards are showing up at shows, antiques
malls, and in price guides.

Steven Heller observed in the distinguished book *School Days,* "Curiously, memories of one's school days tend to be either
overwhelmingly good or bad; no one is indif-

ferent to that period in life, which accounts for why so many of us return decade after decade to their class reunions, or why so many keep souvenirs and mementos of school days forever."

Boy Scouts

Like schooling, scouting is firmly entrenched in the memories of childhood for both boys and girls. Generally, there is a greater demand for Boy Scout items because they have been around and collected for a longer period. However, in the years ahead the interest in Girl Scout artifacts will rise rapidly.

Because the material generated by the scouting movement is so vast, many collectors choose to specialize in a particular area of scouting paper memorabilia such as storybooks, guidebooks, or handbooks. One of the first and most widely distributed of the Boy Scout materials were the colorful adventure books which, for the most part, were unauthorized, but best-sellers among youngsters, nevertheless. There were several hundred such titles in print before 1920. Eventually, concern about the public image caused the Boy Scouts of America organization to go after some publishing houses, and by the early 1920s newly published Boy Scout fiction books were uncommon. Today, many of the editions with strikingly illustrated covers are collected and sometimes used for decorating. They are often in the $6 to $12 range if in good condition.

The first Official *Handbook for Boys* was published in 1912 and had a black-on-brown cover with interwoven blank pages. Later that same year a handbook with a red cover was published. The third edition of the *Handbook For Boys,* issued in 1927, included a Norman Rockwell cover featuring famous Americans. That edition remained in print until 1940 when another Rockwell illustration, this one with a Cub Scout, Boy Scout, and Sea Scout, graced the cover. That same popular illustration was also used for the folding membership cards during the 1940s. Rockwell illus-

trations were used on handbook covers into the 1960s. However, the cover of hiking scouts for the seventh edition in 1965 was drawn by Don Lupo.

Boy Scout merit badge booklets with red-and-white covers appeared during World War II, a photo over a red bottom was used during the 1950s, and a full-cover photo came after that. Cub Scout handbooks, meanwhile, changed dramatically in the 1940s, going from the rather plain Wolf Cub editions to the full faces of the Bear, Lion, and Wolf. After 1948 they were officially known as Cub Scout Books.

Boy's Life, the official publication of the Boy's Scouts of America, was first published in 1911. It was in that magazine that Norman Rockwell established himself as major artist before moving on to the *Saturday Evening Post.* Early issues of *Boy's Life* and those with Rockwell-era covers are currently quite collectible. Rockwell also did some *Boys' Life* covers in the 1940s and 1950s after he had moved to the *Post. Scouting Magazine,* the official publication for adults, first appeared in 1913. For Girl Scouts, *Daisy Magazine* served Brownies and their leaders, and *American Girl* represented older scouts.

In 1985 the Boys Scouts of America celebrated what *USA Today* called "75 years of tying knots, telling creepy stories by the campfire, wearing uniforms and neckerchiefs, helping little old ladies across the street and being prepared for anything. . . ." That same 75th-anniversary year, *Smithsonian Magazine* published an issue with a Boy Scout in full and colorful uniform on the cover, a legitimate scouting collectible in itself today.

Paperback Books

Many things were once abundant in our popular culture before changing dramatically if not fading away entirely. Like comic books, paperback books are a good example of an icon of American culture that is enjoying an afterlife based on the flashy issues of the past. The modern paperback is generally considered to have gotten its start in 1938 with the very limited printing of Pearl Buck's *The Good Earth.* Pocket Books began mass marketing them in 1939, and soon afterwards, several companies were in the same business. The books, measuring roughly 4-by-7 inches, were priced at 25¢—one-tenth of their hardback counterparts—and given blazing covers to attract mostly working- to middle-class males. The books were made relatively cheaply and designed to quickly attract attention (again like comic books) before being tossed aside for the next one. A comparatively limited number of paperbacks survived in reasonable condition because of their disposable nature.

In 1950 Fawcett Publications entered the paperback field with Gold Medal Books. The imprint became highly successful, in part because most of the titles were original rather than being reprints of hardcover books as were the paperbacks of most other publishers at the time. Two years later, Ace Books launched their Ace Double Novels with two pulp-inspired covers instead of one.

Other publishers who joined the paperback market for varying periods of time included Avon, Ballantine, Beacon (one of the most productive and also known for some of the most lurid covers), Black Knight, Bonded Mysteries, Cardinal, Checkerbooks, Crest, Lion Books, Popular Library, Pyramid, Phantom, Signet Books, and Venus Books. Book from many of the paperback publishers are often difficult to locate today because many companies simply went out of business after a few years or were dropped by parent or merging firms. Consequently, some collectors primarily seek the scarce and obscure imprint titles of the 1940s and 1950s.

Cover art was, of course, a major factor in the production of the books. The whole point was to catch the eye of the passerby in the bus terminal or dime store. Early paperback covers were usually inspired by hardcover dust-jacket designs, but gradually they became more realistic and hard-hitting. Many managed to combine splashy colors with partially clad people. Artists frequently did not sign the covers of their work, but those that did included Milton Charles, Leonard Leone, and Cliff Young. Both signed and unsigned covers are currently collectible.

Science fiction paperbacks were one of the first types to be collected. Other areas of interest include adventure, Old West, mystery, early romance, historical, and outrageous—either by cover art or book title, or both. Also collected are paperbacks directly related to movies and TV shows, cartoons and popular comic strips, sports, early editions of modern authors, and those with an African-American connection.

Condition is an increasingly critical factor with paperbacks. Such books are rarely found in just-off-the-rack mint condition. On the other hand, excessive wear severely restricts their collectible value. Early commercial paperbacks were bound in a flexible, plastic-laminated card stock. If the cover was bent too far, the coating easily cracked and cannot be properly repaired. Another problem is loose or lost pages due to cheaply glued bindings. Despite their brilliant color, none of the books were designed to survive much usage, and most did not.

Future Collectibles

From a cultural standpoint, a number of other paper items are also fading from the scene and will likely be eventual collectibles. Sooner or later electronic banking will replace those wonderful and fanciful checks which have been a big part of the 20th-century culture. The experts say checks will be gone at some point, just like paper money once replaced tobacco, corn, and beaver skins in the marketplace. Checks will fall into truncation, meaning they will cease movement after being deposited for the first time. Banks will save money by not handling all those checks, and electronic crediting will replace payroll, dividend, premium, and all other sorts of checks. (How many people actually saved those refund checks from major manufacturers after purchasing a product?) At the payment end, people will use debit cards instead of cash or checks. From an economic standpoint that means debit cards will register banking withdrawals immediately, so nobody can buy groceries on Friday with funds they don't have and make a bank deposit on Monday morning to cover the purchase. From a collecting viewpoint, it means the potential for a dandy collection of checks and related materials.

Besides checks, these disappearing and possibly collectible paper goods also include paper grocery sacks, library catalog cards, materials relating to the draft, Civil Defense signs and pamphlets, black-and-white photos (see Photographs section), fan magazines and record albums (see Entertainment section), paper dolls, telegrams, and stock certificates. Even notepads and cards for playing bridge are on the list of potential collectibles.

Three weeks before the fabled Boston Tea Party in 1773, Samuel Johnson made an interesting notation about what was then a controversial but growing activity: "I am sorry I have not learnt to play at cards," he wrote. "It is very useful in life; it generates kindness and consolidates society." There was a time in this century when cards playing—whether or not it generated kindness and consolidated society—was a part of our culture. Decks of cards were frequently provided aboard passenger trains, commercial airplanes, as premiums from gas stations, and with the purchase of certain products at the market. From the 1930s through the 1950s, there were as many as 40 million bridge players in the United States, and at least that many poker players, who usually played for more than mere points. The best-selling book *Going Going Gone, Vanishing Americana* written in 1994, reported that by the early 1990s there were probably no more than five or six hundred serious college-age bridge players in the U.S. (And where are all the score pads, tally sheets, and other paper products associated with bridge playing?)

As the century comes to a close, however, card games—from bridge to poker—are generally on the decline, as people are more inclined to watch videos or television for entertainment. Playing cards of the past—whether a deck of Fleet Wing gasoline station premiums or some airplane spotter playing cards from World War II provided by Coca-Cola—are a pleasant collectible for today and tomorrow.

Newspapers

It is no longer major news that much of the information once provided by newspapers for public consumption will be available on a more specialized basis along the electronic information highway. In fact, everyone is talking or writing about the demise of the old and the rise of the new. In January 1993 the phrase "information highway," or variations of it, appeared just 57 times in articles stored in the Nexis database of hundreds of newspapers, magazines, and other publications. In January of 1994 it was used 1,480 times by the same basic sources.

Simply put, we are viewing the rising tide of a new form of information transmission which will largely alter the nature of newspapers and magazines. Many will cease to exist in their present state. Moreover, the economics of our culture are as compelling as the electronics. The number of communities served by more than one local newspaper fell from over 500 in the 1920s to under 100 in the 1990s. Correspondingly, newspaper readership has steadily declined since the late 1960s. Barely half of the country's adults read a newspaper on a daily basis, and those that do are usually older people. Younger generations have grown up relying on television for their information, if they rely on anything at all.

In the next decade, as the world welcomes more computers, cable channels, and phone lines along the information highway, the few surviving traditional newspapers and magazines will be increasingly viewed as collectible. Right now the century's most collectible newspaper is probably one dealing with early flight. One edition in particular carried a headline declaring, "Huge kite soars above the Carolina coast, machine that can really fly." The date was 1903 and the event was the first manned flight by the

Wright brothers. There are different versions of this newspaper, and the better ones now go for $500 to $700 each, in good condition. Running a close second among the most collectible newspapers of the 20th century is probably the famed *Chicago Tribune* blooper-headline issue of 1948 proclaiming "Dewey Defeats Truman." Those papers referring to President Truman's election bring prices of $200 to $500 and sometimes more. Also high on the most-wanted list are newspapers headlining the historic sinking of the Titanic in 1912.

Most collectible newspapers of the 20th century, and even many from the 19th century, are priced considerably less than those cited above. Among the current popular categories are American presidents, wars, gangsters of the 1920s and 1930s, Old West, sports, and superstars. A Memphis newspaper reporting the death of Elvis Presley in that city in 1977 is valued at $40 or more, about four times the price of the same account in another city's newspaper. Newspapers reporting the 1941 World War II attack on Pearl Harbor are often in the $30 to $50 range, but the *Honolulu Star-Bulletin*'s headlined account is worth several hundred dollars. (See also the Household, Sports, and Political sections.)

Generally, the most collectible 20th-century newspapers—which, by the way, are considered by many to be quite underpriced because collecting them is relatively new— are from larger cities rather than small towns and have larger, screaming headlines rather than smaller ones. Aside from breaking major news stories, some newspapers are being collected simply because of their Old West atmosphere or because of interest in the obscure communities served by weekly newspapers in the 1950s. Through news accounts, advertisements, and sometimes illustrations or photographs, newspapers depict everyday life as it was and as it was lived by citizens of the community.

Today, collectible newspapers are sometimes sold in groups. An assortment of 15 or 20 newspapers from the 1960s featuring John

Kennedy and the Moon Landing might list between $50 and $100. A similar-sized group of World War II newspapers with coverage of key events such as the death of Franklin Roosevelt and the Japanese surrender may have a package price of $100 to $150. Newspapers detailing the Vietnam war, with great collecting potential, can be located for considerably less.

Condition, of course, is always important. Prior to the 1880s newspapers were composed of material with high rag and cotton fiber content. Shortly before the turn of the century, printers began to frequently use wood pulps with their accompanying acids. As a result, older newspapers of the Civil War era and before are often in much better condition than those printed within the past 100 years. Collectors also need to be wary of reproductions of famous newspapers. Large numbers of reprints exist of the January 4, 1800, *Ulster County Gazette* dealing with the death of George Washington and the April 25, 1865, *New York Herald* detailing the death of Abraham Lincoln. Usually such reprints are on an inferior quality paper.

Magazines

Old magazines, and those that are not so old, are also becoming widespread popular culture collectibles. Consider, for example, that *TV Guides* had no following at all not too many years ago. (See sections on Household and Entertainment.) "In the not too distant future, magazines will be a very established medium of collecting our culture," according to one leading dealer and collector in California. "They are a perfect representation of our immediate past, they are portable and framable, and they are a small type of investment that appreciates over the years."

Already many magazines also have considerable crossover value. People who collect just Elvis Presley items, Western movie heroes, cartoon shows, or Lucille Ball become part of the ground swell. For example, a 1953 issue of *TV Digest and Guide* (a forerunner of *TV Guide*) with Lucy's neighbors on the cover now lists at $100.

Magazines with coverage of space flights, Vietnam, 1960s television, Watergate, fashions, and various social changes are already moving into some collectible circles. As an illustration, for some years the demand has grown for the early 1950s news magazines, including *Time, Newsweek,* and *U.S. News & World Report.* Newsmakers of that era who adorned these covers included Harry Truman, Dwight Eisenhower, Douglas McArthur, and Eleanor Roosevelt. For years magazine advertising has been a solid field of paper collecting (see Advertising section) and will continue to provide a fine source of informative and decorative material for future generations.

Cereal Boxes

When it comes down to it, paper collectibles of popular culture can include any number of absorbing things, even cereal boxes. These containers have long been valued among sports fans, e.g., Wheaties, Breakfast of Champions (see Sports section), but the fascination has gone quite beyond that.

Popular cereals of the 1960s and early 1970s with cartoon characters and premiums can be quite collectible. In recent years a box of Kellogg's Corn Flakes drew considerable interest. The 1984 box contained a color photo of Vanessa Williams during her brief term as Miss America. If you recall, when nude photographs of her were published in *Penthouse* magazine, the "exposure" cost her the title—the first time in history a Miss America was dethroned under such circumstances. The unusual box sold for $60 at a national collectibles auction. And finally, the experts say cereal boxes containing the original cereal are more valuable than empty or flattened ones.

RECOMMENDED READING

Huxford's Paperback Value Guide by Bob and Sharon Huxford, Collector Books.
Going Going Gone, Vanishing Americana by Susan Jonas and Marilyn Nissenson, Chronicle Books.

PRICE LISTINGS

Advertising flyer, Tex Family Barber Shop, adults 50¢, children 35¢, 1930s, 4 × 7, $6

Annual, *Star Trek,* hardcover, comic book style, 1973, British, 80 pages, $32

Book from Burma-Shave, *Verse By the Side of the Road,* story of signs and jingles, 10th printing, 1973, hardcover, 5 × 8, $15

Bookmark, Mr. Peanut, New York World's Fair, 1939, 3 × 6, fine condition, $25

Catalog, *Standard Surgical Instruments,* J.F. Hartz, Detroit, 1922, illustrated, 416 pages, $30

Cereal box, Kellogg's Corn Flakes, 1984, Vanessa Williams, Miss America, $60

Check, business woman, Mary Williams, retail and wholesale lumber, 1880s, $10

Lady and the Tramp, *hardcover, Simon & Schuster, 1955. Photo courtesy of Hake's Americana & Collectibles.*

Broadside poster for lecture by Kit Carson, Jr., 1872. Photo courtesy of Swann Galleries, Inc.

Coloring book, *Dennis the Menace,* 1962, Watkins-Strathmore, 80 pages, 8 × 11, $35

Color-by-number book, *Family Affair,* 1969, Whitman, some wear, 8 × 15, $35

Comic book, *Adventures of Big Boy* (restaurant), issue no. 199, 1973, very fine condition, $12.50

Graduation program, Shenandoah Valley Academy class of 1920, New Market, Virginia, 3 × 5, $7

Hardcover book, *Lady and the Tramp,* 1955, Simon & Schuster, 28 pages, 9.5 × 12.5, $9

Lecture poster, Kit Carson, 1872, 29.5 × 10.5, $330

Magazine, *Crime Does Not Pay,* Starkweather case, 1969, pulp-style cover, $8

Magazine, *Life,* Judy Garland cover, December 1944, $25

Magazine, *Playboy,* March 1965, Vargas cover, $8

Magazine, *Saturday Evening Post,* barber and customer, Norman Rockwell cover, May 18, 1940, $28

Crime Does Not Pay *magazine, December, 1969, Starkweather cover.*

Life magazine, Judy Garland cover, 1944. *Photo courtesy of Hake's Americana & Collectibles.*

Magazine, *Saturday Evening Post,* Draft dodgers, anti-Vietnam cover article, "Hell No, We Won't Go," January 27, 1968, $20

Magazine, *Scientific American,* battleship cover, Paris Exposition, September 1900, $15

Magazine, *Western Family Magazine,* Disney's Bongo Bear cover, June 1947, mint condition, $27.50

Membership manual, official Captain Midnight manual and code book, 1940–1941, $100

Menu, Savarin, railroad station restaurant, 1938, Pittsburgh, Pennsylvania, $10

Model box, Star Wars R2-D2, MPC Model, 1977, 20th Century Fox, mint parts, 6 × 10, $28

Newspaper, "Titanic Sinks," *New York Times,* April 16, 1912, $265

Playboy *magazine, March 1965. Photo courtesy of Hake's Americana & Collectibles.*

Official Captain Midnight secret code book and membership manual, 1940–1941. Photo courtesy of Hake's Americana & Collectibles.

Star Wars R2-D2 model, box and unused parts, 1977. Photo courtesy of Hake's Americana & Collectibles.

Paperback book, *Free Ride,* 1957, James Fox, Popular Library, good condition, $3

Paperback book, *Tillie,* 1952, David Westheimer, Pyramid, good condition, $6.50

Paperback book, *The 24th Horse,* 1946, Hugh Pentecost, Popular Library, very good condition, $15

Penny arcade cards, Western movie stars, set of 32, 1940s, $28

Playing cards, Coca-Cola airplane spotter, ca. 1943, boxed, $100

Poster, Louis Farrakhan, "Power at Last," 1985, Richard Jones Armory, full color, 21 × 22, $22

Program, Folies Bergère, musical review in Paris, 1931, color and sepia, 24 pages, $50

Newspaper, "Titanic Sinks," 1912, New York Times.

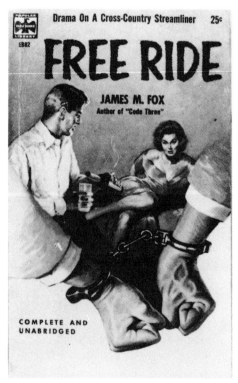

Paperback novel by James Fox, Eagle Books, 1957.

Folies Bergère program, Paris, 1931. Photo courtesy of Hake's Americana & Collectibles.

Marksmanship booklet, Boy Scouts of America, 1953.

Road map, "Official Illinois State Highway Map," 1956, fine condition, $15

Scouting booklet, *Marksmanship,* Boy Scouts of America, 1953, $6

Sheet music, "Pussyfoot Fox Trot" by Slap White, 1915, Frank K. Root and Co., Chicago, $5

Specialty book, *Yankee Denim Dandies* by Barber Fisher, history of blue jeans, denim cover, 1974, 8 × 11, $22.50

Steamship menu, S.S. *Tutshi,* White Pass & Yukon Route, northwest coast, ca. 1915, $12.50

Sticker, "Eighth Wisconsin Radio/Music Expo," 1930, Milwaukee, red, white with radio air waves, 1.5 × 2, $11

Telephone book, Hotel Thunder Bird, Las Vagas, Nevada, simulated leather cover, 9 advertising pages, 1960s, $25

Transit pass, Los Angeles, with Sheriff's Championship Rodeo promotion, Roy Rogers, 1948, 2.5 × 4, $32

"Pussyfoot Fox Trot" sheet music, started fox trot dance craze, 1915, issued by Frank K. Root & Co., Chicago.

Northern Pacific travel booklet, 64 pages, 1930s.

Van Briggle Art Pottery tourist guide, Colorado Springs, Colorado, 1930s.

Travel booklet, *Northern Pacific Railway,* 1930s, red cover, 64 pages, $30

Visitor pamphlet, Van Briggle Art Pottery, Colorado Springs, Colorado, multicolor, 1930s, $24

Window card, "We Gave For Our Own—For Our Allies," red, white and blue, eagle design, World War II, 4 × 5, $7.50

Workbook, *Dick and Jane, Think & Do Book,* softcover, 1946, red and blue cover, Scott, Foresman & Company, 8 × 11, $18

POSTCARDS

Everybody knows about postcards. We have grown up with them, and our parents and grandparents grew up with them. We have stuffed them in drawers, mounted them in scrapbooks, and stored them away in old shoe boxes. From time to time in the 20th century, the experts have predicted the death of the postcard as a medium of communication, and they have been wrong. It has helped that no subject is too trivial or trite to picture on a postcard—from main street to meandering ducks. As a consequence, anyone now collecting anything can find a few topical postcards to fit the category.

Even today in the midst of the electronic era and the information highway, Americans use 500 million postcards every year for advertising, political campaigns, as remainders of dental visits, and just to show where the last vacation was spent.

The marketplace is a challenge, too. A scene from the beach at Atlantic City may be worth a dollar or two, but an old fire truck or trolley car may be worth considerably more. In 1990 a collector/dealer in Macon, Georgia, paid $12,500 for one of only five known advertising postcards for Waverly Cycles. The cards came from an 1898 Art Nouveau poster created by artist Alphonse Mucha for a U.S. bicycle manufacturer that had a branch in Paris. This particular postcard had not been used, written on, or mailed. Earlier that same year it had been purchased in Paris by two Connecticut dealers who, in turn, sold it to new owners in Georgia.

No one knows exactly how many other unknown and undiscovered Waverly Cycles advertising postcards are still out there. Finding one in an old box of cards, within the pages of a Victorian book, or in a flea market assortment may not change your life, as the lottery sales slogan goes, but it could sure make your day. One dealer who was involved in the sales transaction of one of the world's most valuable postcards, told a newspaper reporter that some top-of-the-line postcards are rarer than stamps or coins. Not only is the postcard game not over, said the dealer, it hasn't even started yet.

Of course, not all postcards are valuable, or even close to it. Generally, the best are those produced between the 1890s and World War II, that have remained in wonderful condition, and have some political or social significance. On the other hand, it is not simply a matter of age or historical trappings. A McDonald's promotional postcard from the 1960s featuring a 15¢ hamburger lists at around $11 currently and will probably go higher in the years ahead.

Postcards are one of the unique paper antiques that can be found anywhere, from the local flea market to the lofty Swann Galleries in New York. Swann's, not surprisingly, deals only in the more valuable cards. Bidders at a typical Swann sale paid $1,100 for a postcard supporting the campaign of James Cox of Ohio, who ran for president in 1920 with Franklin Roosevelt as his running mate. The card's slogan was "Be Cox Sure in November." During the same month at Swann's, a campaign puzzle postcard from the 1908 Taft campaign brought $660 and five jumbo hold-to-light cards from the 1904 Louisiana Purchase Exposition sold for $1,650.

One of the first illustrated postcards was introduced at the 1893 Chicago Columbian Exposition and World's Fair and featured a scene that included the exposition hall. By 1907 the U.S. government had agreed to allow handwritten messages on the address side of the card, just in case a picture was not

enough. At the time, postcards sold for about a penny, and they could be mailed for another penny. People loved them so much, they also kept them in albums with their precious family photographs. By 1909 Americans were buying more than one billion postcards every year.

Scenic Postcards

Many publishers were already making a substantial profit from postal greeting cards, but they wisely saw the economic opportunity in expanding to picture postcards. Ironically, the booming enterprise of marketing these artful views also served to preserve in color some community sites that would have otherwise likely gone unrecorded, at least unrecorded in the "revolutionary" art of color photography.

Main Street was probably the very thing that caused the Detroit Publishing Company to prosper. They were one of the nation's leading postcard publishers at the turn of the century. The keystone of the company's success was pioneer American photographer William Jackson, who joined the company in 1898. Not only did Jackson bring with him 10,000 glass-plate negatives, but he had other company photographers travel widely taking their own photos and purchasing stock from local photographers to build the company's supply of images. In the midst of the Main Street postcard wars of the early 1900s, Detroit Publishing Company had more than 25,000 original photographs available, along with a distribution system that included worldwide retail and mail-order sales, as well as racks at resorts and tourist attractions.

For more than half a century, travel postcards provided ever-mobile Americans with a permanent view of where they had been. Usually there was a vast array to select from at major tourist sites, such as national parks, major cities, and historic locations. Postcards could truly be from anywhere—Hoke's Truck Stop on the four-lane at Marietta, Georgia, or greetings from the heart of the Orange Empire in Santa Ana, California. Some of the most popular travel postcards were those with large letters spelling out greetings. Each letter in the location's name provided a view of a local monument or building. During the 1940s and 1950s over 1,000 cites, sites, and states were eventually portrayed on the cards which were primarily printed by Curt Teich Company.

Photo Postcards

Besides the colorfully printed ones, a few tourist hot spots—such as the Ozarks, the Wisconsin Dells, Smokey Mountain National Park, and Key West, Florida—began offering actual photographs on postcards in the 1950s. They were starkly attractive in glossy black and white. In the long run, the real photo travel postcards were far fewer in number than regular postcards, mainly because they were more costly to produce. Consequently, they are somewhat higher on the travel-card collectibility scale.

Real photo postcards have become one of the strongest attractions in the postcard field because they are the closest to authentic. The major breakthrough for cards of this type came in 1902 when the Eastman Kodak Company began offering postcard-size photographic paper, which allowed photographs to be printed directly from negatives rather than involving a printing press. This innovation not only allowed regional companies to produce real photo postcards, but put neighborhood photographers directly in the postcard business as well. As early as 1903 the *British Journal of Photography* suggested there was real money to be made with this process: "The best subjects for regular sales are the stock views of the town, the principal business thoroughfares, public buildings, and chief residential roads. The latter especially are growing in importance as the postcard cult spreads, for people who have met at holiday resorts and wish to exchange greetings through the post, they like to have a view of their own road, if such happens to present a good appearance."

The photographic paper and, therefore, the cards themselves bore the familiar names of Kodak, Ansco, or some other supplier. Today many of the photo cards can be identified by such marks on the reverse side as EKC, AZOA, VELOZ, KRUXO, CYKO, DARKO, EEKP, NOKO, and DOPS. From 1906 through 1910 the Kodak company added to the specialty by providing mail-order prints of postcards from photographer's negatives for only a few cents a card. Starting in 1912 people could purchase machines like the Diamond Post Card Gun, manufactured by the International Metal and Ferrotype Company, which took "postcard pictures direct on the positive paper in four sizes." Their advertisements claimed five to eight clear pictures per minute, "finished on the spot. Postcards sell at ten cents each and you make eight cents net profit on every dime. It's the biggest money maker you ever heard of at bathing beaches, ball parks, carnivals, and fairs." All of these creative sources combined to give the country a vast variety of real photo postcards, especially prior to World War I.

In effect, almost anyone with a camera could technically produce a real photo postcard of anything from a disaster to a local railroad operation to a visiting celebrity. Real photo postcards continued to be produced through the 1940s and early 1950s, although at that point they were typically marketed in a particular tourist area by publishers like W.M. Cline Company of Chattanooga, Tennessee, or L.L. Cook Company of Milwaukee, Wisconsin. Most of these were identified on the reverse as photograph cards. Today a majority of real photo postcards are available to collectors in the $8 to $16 range, with some nondescript subjects valued lower. Topics with greater worth include large-image automobiles, trucks with advertising, farm equipment, fire trucks, train depots, trolley cars, airplanes, Indians, horse-drawn vehicles, business interiors, and exaggerated scenes with photo credit lines of Frank Conrad or William Martin. In 1993 Swann Gallery sold a group of 17 real photo postcards for more than $400. The lot included photos of blacks, costumed circus performers, store interiors, and county fairs.

For the most part, the majority of postcards from the first half of the 20th century, other than greeting cards, were known as view cards. They evolved from black and white in the early days through various stages of color, much like motion pictures. The color process, of course, proved to be a financial boon to publishers. Although many types of color printing were used, the authochrome process is generally considered the first practical system of color photography. It was finally marketed in 1907 after some years of refinement. The basic color screen system of authochrome remained popular on cards well into the 1930s.

Other Collecting Categories

While Main Street was a major attraction on early postcards, collectors who followed many generations later were more interested in the views of transportation of that era. Airplanes, trains, trucks, boats, ships, balloons, and even bicycles are solid favorites in printed cards, as they are in real photo cards. Stores and shops from 1900 to 1920, especially showing people at work, and business district scenes, especially from the smaller cities and towns, are quite collectible. Buildings, churches, schools, and courthouses are found in greater numbers than just about any other views and are usually sold for just a few dollars each. At one time in America, every town had a courthouse or similar governmental building, and nearby was a five-and-dime store with a rack of the courthouse postcards. By the middle of the 1950s, such cards were not nearly as readily available as they had been before, and tourists had to rely more and more on major tourist attractions and buildings of larger cities. Individual establishments in the 1950s and 1960s, such as drugstores, restaurants, or motels, might sponsor their own card to be given away to customers or sold for a few cents. But, in the end, it was usually the grand hotel, hospital, university, or metropolis that became the source of such postcards.

Disasters and other special newsworthy events are snapped up today by collectors, just as they were by curious citizens when the events occurred. Often these event cards were printed in black and white and gave fine visual portrayals to generations whose only other immediate reference was newspapers. The best of the rest may well be dogs and cats, children (especially on cards celebrating various holidays), amusement parks and fairs, entertainment personalities, political candidates, and, as with real photo cards, those with ethnic depictions of African-Americans or American Indians.

Another category of collecting early postcards is by artist, many of who signed prominently across the bottom of their holiday greeting or simple sketch. From Jules Charles Aviat to Bernhardt Wall, artists' names can be significant. Among those with premium value are Ellen Clapsaddle, Frances Brundage, Herman Kaulback, Paul Hagemans, Norman Rockwell, H.B. Griggs, Grace Drayton, Bertha Corbell, R.F. Outcault, and Harrison Fisher, creator of one of the most popular images in America during the early 20th century—the Fisher Girls. Fisher depicted lovely women in various activities, such as on a buggy ride, reading, painting, shopping, or at a wedding. Many of the ladies were shown with charming and fashionable hats, and the hats became almost a signature for Fisher, whose works adorned hundreds of different postcards from 1905 through 1912.

Collecting Tips

Victorians at the turn of the century used New Year's Day postcards to decorate their homes for holiday parties. Over the years postcards commemorating St. Patrick's Day, Valentine's Day, Halloween, Thanksgiving, and Christmas were used in similar fashion. Flashy travel postcards also have decorating appeal. In the Simon and Schuster book *Designing With Collectibles,* author Candace Manroe depicts an entire rack of travel postcards as they might have appeared in a store during the 1950s. According to Manroe, "Ephemera such as travel postcards, many of which are highly colorful and richly illustrated, add an offbeat splash of character to a room."

And while the heyday of the postcard may have been the turn of the century, there are many fine examples around the country of white bordered cards printed between 1915 and 1930. Cards from the linen era—the 1930s through the 1940s—are also abundant. These cards were printed on paper with a high rag content, giving them a linenlike finish. Most cards produced after World War II are considered to be part of the photochrome era.

The best advice on collecting any style or type of postcards is to strive for the best quality available. One or two postcards in pristine condition are better than a dozen in poorer condition.

A final note: Unlike most paper antiques which are usually collected long after they are no longer being produced, postcards have been around for 100 years, are still being manufactured today, and are available from a wealth of sources. One young mother I know has started a collection of contemporary advertising postcards for her three-year-old son. He loves sorting through them and has learned to identify the majority of products and companies on sight.

RECOMMENDED READING

The Postcard Price Guide by J.L. Mashburn, Colonial House.
The Official Price Guide to Postcards by Diane Allmen, House of Collectibles.
The Postcard Collector Magazine, PO Box 337, Iola, WI 54945.

Christmas postcard by Ellen Clapsaddle, 1913.

PRICE LISTINGS

Advertising, McDonald's, 15¢ hamburger, 1960s, $11

Amusement park, Dream City, black and white, early 1900s, Wilkinsburg, Pennsylvania, $6

Artist signed, Frances Brundage, Halloween greetings, ca. 1909, $16

Artist signed, Ellen Clapsaddle, red-suited Santa, ca. 1913, $12

Amusement park, early 1900s, Wilkinsburg, Pennsylvania.

Advertising postcard, 1903, by R.F. Outcault.

Artist signed, Harrison Fisher, "My Lady Awaits," 1907, $16

Artist signed, R.F. Outcault, 1903, Banner Buggy Company, $12

Billy Graham crusade, 1960s, Charlotte, North Carolina, color, $2

Black, two boys in raggedy clothing, color tinted, 1920s, $4

Black, young caddy with golf clubs, ca. 1907, $12

Christmas greeting postcard, Santa in red suit, unsigned, 1920s, $3

Comic postcard, beach scene, 1940s, unsigned, color, $1

Entertainment, Elvis Presley, promoting two films, British, full color, 1960s, $5

Exploration, Polar Expedition of Dr. Fridtjof Nansen, set of 12, chromolithographed, original paper folder, ca. 1898, $467

Exposition, Columbian Exposition, Chicago, three color views of exposition, 1893, $110

Exposition, Panama-Pacific Exposition, 1915, color, $6

Farm threshing scene, color tinted, early 1900s, Oxnard, California, $10

Halloween, artist John Winsch, unsigned, sleeping maiden, 1911, $70

Horse-drawn log wagon, real photo, 1916, Franklin, Indiana, $5

Military, Camp Atterbury (Ind.), army barracks, linen, 1940s, $3

Elvis Presley movie postcard from England, 1960s.

Halloween, 1911, John Winsch (unsigned), sleeping maiden.

Comic postcard, 1940s, beach scene.

Real photo, horse-drawn log wagon, 1916.

Military, Japanese troops, World War II, color, printed in Japan, $10

Motel, Air Park Model, Mexico, Missouri, linen, unused, 1940s, $5

Ocean liner, Cunard Line, early 1900s, Raphael Tuck, $6

Ocean liner, Cunard Line, *Queen Elizabeth,* color, British, $5

Patriotic theme, "Our Country and Our Flag," early 1900s, full color, $3.50

Police officer on horseback, New York City, full color, early 1900s, $4

Political, Eugene V. Debs for President, Socialist Party, real photo portrait card, unused, $825

Political, President Lyndon Johnson, full color, 1960s, $3

Lyndon Johnson presidential postcard, full color, 1960s.

Political, Cox-Roosevelt campaign, "Be Cox Sure in November," rare, 1920, $1,100

Promotional, Beatles, Concert Tour Advertising Ltd., pictures group, ca. 1963, $4

Railroad, Pittsburg & Lake Erie Railroad, New York City train, Youngstown, Ohio, 1950s, $4

Patriotic theme, early 1900s, "Our Country and Our Flag," full color.

Unused real photo postcard with Teddy Roosevelt and Hoxsey in biplane, 1910. Photo courtesy of Swann Galleries, Inc.

Real photo, Boy Scouts, 1913, Camp Sheridan.

Women's basketball team, real photo, dated 1912.

Real photo postcard, Teddy Roosevelt in biplane, Cole and Company, unused, 1910, $192

Real photo postcard, biplane, 1910, Douglas, Arizona, $15

Real photo postcard, Boy Scouts, Camp Sheridan, 1913, $10

Real photo postcard, peanut vendor, ca. 1912, $6

Real photo postcard, truck stop, 1940s, Marietta, Georgia, $4

Real photo postcard, fantasy airplane, man and woman flying, France, ca. 1910, $20

Real photo postcard, Victorian home, 1907, Mt. Pleasant, Iowa, $15

Real photo postcard, sports, girls' basketball team, black and white, 1912, $20

Street scene, 1920s, Macon, Georgia, $3

Swimming suits, two women at the beach, black and white, 1906, $2

Thanksgiving, turkey, signed "Ellen Clapsaddle," 1912, $5

Trolley cars, Canal Street, New Orleans, Louisiana, 1915, color, $6

Transportation, Dallas Municipal Airport, Love Field, Dallas, Texas, linen, 1940s, $8

Travel, "Thru New Mexico to Painted Desert, Petrified Forest," folder of 18 views, ca. 1936, $7.50

Real photo, 1940s truck stop, black and white, Marietta, Georgia.

Swimsuits, 1906, women at the beach.

SPORTS

One beautiful summer day, my daughter and I ventured into the hinterlands in search of great undiscovered garage sales only the nearest neighbors would know about. It was too early for any of the day's garage sales when we reached one small crossroads, but the town library was open for business. It appeared to us that they were selling every single book in the place, although, in reality, they were undoubtedly just making room for new books.

At any rate, the lawn and sidewalks were covered with books, and, fortunately, they were arranged in sections much like the library inside must have been. I went directly to the sports section and gathered up two large stacks. The people conducting the sale furnished grocery bags for the purchases and sold them filled for 25¢ each.

Most of the sports books I had found had been there since the 1950s and 1960s and probably hadn't been checked out in decades. Without boasting about each and every

Babe Ruth in New York Yankees uniform with Louisville Slugger.

title, it is enough to say that *Connie Mack's Baseball Book,* issued in 1950 by Alfred Knopf, was signed neatly and beautifully by the author. (We found out later that when it was first printed that particular book had been a gift to a nearby elementary school and was later passed on to the town library.) The point is that treasures are still out there, especially in the case of sports memorabilia, since there is such an enormous variety of paper materials.

Sports collectors can look for programs, tickets, pocket schedules, posters, magazines, or even old library books. Additionally, there are magazine advertisements from throughout the 20th century, yearbooks, media guides, newspapers, cereal boxes, newspapers, press passes, and more. There are so many categories to chose from that the potential collector may want to consult some reference books, such as *Sports Collectibles Value Guide* by Roderick Malloy from Wallace-Homestead Book Company. Malloy lists thousands upon thousands of sports items.

Many years ago at an auction I purchased an early 20th-century scrapbook for less than $5. The previous owner had pasted all manner of colorful paper items inside, from early Christmas gift tags to engraved business cards. On one of the many pages were two neatly attached orange ticket stubs for the 1914 Indianapolis 500 Mile Race. They remained in the scrapbook, filed away in a trunk, until Malloy's book was published. He listed those raincheck tickets at over $200 each. Armed with that information on the marketplace, it was very easy to find a buyer.

Clearly, the great majority of people love sports, and it is not surprising that while there is more paper sports memorabilia out there than most any other collectibles category, there are also more potential collectors. The vast majority of what is collected today is from the professional sports level; however, college sports paper collectibles are steadily gaining in popularity.

Baseball is far ahead of every other sport in the collectibles field and has long held that honor. Each year major league baseball has a paid attendance of nearly 54 million, according to the *Statistical Abstract of the United States*. No wonder it has such a following in the collector field. Next in annual attendance figures are college football with 35.5 million and college basketball with 32.5 million. Interestingly, however, college sports have yet to reach the heights of the collecting popularity of professional football.

Pro football has annual ticket sales of a mere 17 million, but they have the Super Bowl, of course, which has 130 million viewers, the largest annual audience of anything on television in America. The Super Bowl pales in comparison, however, to the World Cup Soccer play-offs, which reportedly have a worldwide TV audience of nearly two billion.

Behind pro football in fan attendance is professional basketball at 14 million and hockey at 13.7 million. Obviously, these areas of sports memorabilia will prove to have a significant growth in the number of collectors in the future.

On the other hand, a wise collector or investor might be spending some time at the racetrack, not betting on the longshots but gathering up programs, tickets, and such. Nearly 70 million people a year pay to get into horse-racing events, besting baseball and college sports. Even greyhound racing has annual crowds of 26.4 million—higher attendance than professional football, basketball, or hockey.

It is probably a fair assessment to predict that the great American pastime of baseball will have lots of company in the years ahead in terms of potential fans and collectors. Not only will some of those sports begin to spawn more collectors, but also the collectibility future of also-ran sports, minorities in sports, and women in sports (especially those relatively few women featured prior to the 1960s) will be bright indeed.

Sports memorabilia made of paper is to be found everywhere, from garage sales to the glitzy auction galleries of New York City. A friend of mine was scouting out suburban

garage sales one Saturday morning and mentioned his interest in sports memorabilia. The lady next door, who was not having the sale but was helping out, asked if he was interested in sports magazines. She led the eager customer to a basement where about two decades of *Sports Illustrated* magazines were neatly stacked on the shelves, along with a sprinkling of other sports magazines and sports programs. Her sons, now grown and gone, had faithfully gathered them during their childhood years, and she was glad to have them cleaned out. The price for all was $2.

Given the changing character of the collectibles business in America, it is no longer surprising to see some of the nation's leading auction houses routinely handle paper sports memorabilia. From Christie's, Sotheby's, and Swann's in New York City to Butterfield & Butterfield's in San Francisco, with a stop at Treadway Gallery in Cincinnati along the way—all have issued catalogs from time to time dominated by sports collectibles.

Probably the heaviest sports memorabilia hitter among the general auction galleries is Guernsey's of New York. Their major sports collectibles auctions handle more than 2,000 lots and amount to more than $2 million dollars in sales. Sporting auction catalogs, available from Guernsey's at $25 each, have nearly 200 pages, are fully illustrated, and offer pre-sale price estimates. Write Guernsey's at 108½ East 73rd Street, New York, NY 10021 or call (212) 794-2280.

At this writing, the leader of strictly sports memorabilia auction houses is Leland's Collectibles, 245 Fifth Avenue, Suite 902, New York, NY 10016, phone (212) 545-0800. Those who attend Leland's gala events can expect to see 500 to 1,000 lots which include items such as an 8-by-10-inch photo signed by Babe Ruth in the $3,000 to $4,000 range or a canceled bank check signed by Jackie Robinson in 1948 for $500 to $600. There is always an amazing assortment of letterheads, contracts, lineup cards, programs, trading cards, and other material. Once Leland's even sold a wrapper from a candy bar endorsed by the great Ruth himself. It was not the Baby Ruth bar, which was, at least technically, named for a child in the White House, but rather a Ruth's Home Run. The wrapper from the 1920s with a full-color photo of the Babe's head brought more than $1,000.

One thing that caught many collectors by surprise is the fact that now even the price guides which reported values on baseball cards and such have collectability. In 1989 I wrote an article for *Beckett's Baseball Guide Monthly* about world series programs. I put aside a copy because of the article and not because Nolan Ryan was featured on the cover. That issue is already listed in some price guides, and several early Beckett's issues have been featured at major auctions. Someday the Ryan cover magazine will be worth much more than what I was paid for the article.

The immortal Babe Ruth probably offered the best conclusion in *The Babe Ruth Story:* "A man who has put away his baseball togs after an eventful life in the game must live on his memories, some good, some bad."

That is, after all, what sports memorabilia on paper amounts to—memories (hopefully, mostly good).

RECOMMENDED READING

Value Guide to Baseball Collectibles by Donald and Craig Raycraft, Collector Books.

Malloy's Sports Collectibles Value Guide by Roderick Malloy, Wallace-Homestead Company.

PRICE LISTINGS

Auto Racing

Postcard, Jimmy Snyder, 1938 championship race, Syracuse, New York, $15

Press kit, 1989 Kodak NASCAR event, with 8 × 10 photos, $25

Program, 1956, Indianapolis 500 Mile Race, $28

Rain check ticket stub, 1914 Indianapolis 500 Mile Race, $220

Baseball

Advertisement, 1962, Roger Maris for Camel Cigarettes, 10 × 13, $10

Book, hardcover, 1950, *My 66 Years in the Big Leagues* by Connie Mack, $28

Book, hardcover, 1950, *Connie Mack's Baseball Book* (autographed copy), $300

Book, hardcover, 1969, *Young Sportsman's Guide to Baseball* by Clary Anderson, $25

Auto racing postcard, 1938, featuring Jimmy Snyder, winner of 100-mile championship race, Syracuse, New York.

Official program for the 500-mile race in Indianapolis, Indiana, 1956.

Comic book, 1979, Dodgers with Sandy
Koufax, $10

Guest pass, 1962 World Series, New
York Yankees vs. San Francisco
Giants, game five, $55

Magazine, *Boys Life,* 1959, Mickey
Mantle cover, $20

Magazine, *Sport,* 1971, Ted Williams
cover, $12

Magazine, *Sports Illustrated,* 1981, Tom
Seaver cover, $7

Newspaper, July 12, 1933, *San Francisco
Chronicle,* "DiMaggio Hits in 47th
Straight Game," $75

Newspaper, June 3, 1941, *Chicago
Tribune,* "Lou Gehrig, Former
Yankee Star, Dies at 37," $150

Newspaper, 1990, *USA Today,* "Ryan
Joins The 300 Club," $5

Opening day, full ticket, 1967, New
York Giants, $35

Photograph, 1935, Babe Ruth with fans,
silver print, $330 (Swann Galleries)

Photograph, 1948, Babe Ruth's farewell
signed by photographer Nat Fein,
$935 (Swann Galleries)

Sports Illustrated, *Tom Seaver cover, July 1981.*

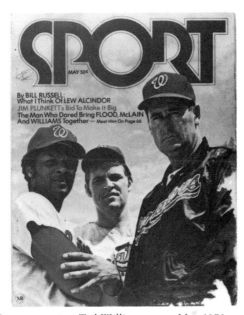

Sport *magazine, Ted Williams cover, May 1971.*

Babe Ruth with fans, silver print, 1935. Photo
courtesy of Swann Galleries, Inc.

Photo of Babe Ruth's farewell appearance, 1948,
by Pulitzer Prize winner Nat Fein. Photo courtesy
of Swann Galleries, Inc.

Mickey Mantle, 1966 wire photo, Mayo Clinic.

Photograph, wire service, 1966, Mickey Mantle, $25

Postcard, 1970s, National Baseball Hall of Fame, George Lange Kelly, $3.50

Price guide, *Beckett's Baseball Card Monthly,* no. 55, 1989, Nolan Ryan cover, $8

Program, 1926 World Series, Yankees vs. Cardinals, $1,500

Program, 1934 World Series, Detroit vs. St. Louis, $400

Record books, 1953 World Series, Gillette Razor Co., $25

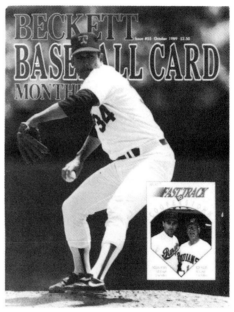

Beckett Baseball Card Monthly, *Nolan Ryan cover, 1989.*

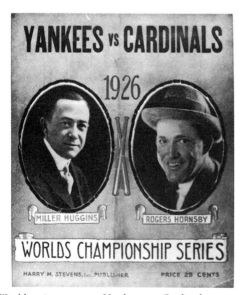

World series program, Yankees vs. Cardinals, 1926.

Baseball Hall of Fame postcard, 1970s, Cooperstown, New York.

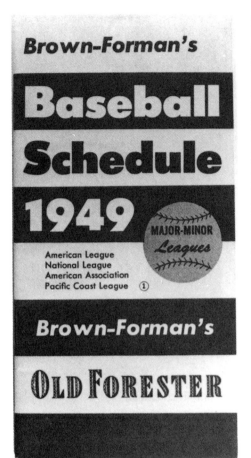

Baseball schedule, 1949, Brown-Forman's Old Forester.

World Champion Cincinnati Reds, 1976, score book.

Schedule booklet, 1949, Brown-Forman's major-minor leagues, with tribute to Babe Ruth who died previous season, $25

Score book, 1976 world champion Cincinnati Reds, $18

Scorecard, 1883, Brown vs. Harvard, players' names printed, $55 (Swann Galleries)

Scorecard/program, 1946, Milwaukee Braves, very good condition, $20

Spring training player roster, 1942, St. Louis Cardinals, $45

Wheaties cereal box back, 1937, Carl Hubbell, $42

Carl Hubbell, Wheaties cereal box back, 1937. Photo courtesy of Hake's Americana & Collectibles.

Basketball

Game pass for official, 1953, Minneapolis Lakers vs. College All-Stars, mint condition, $50

Hardcover book, 1966, *Practical Modern Basketball* by John Wooden, Ronald Press, $15

Magazine, 1961, *Dell Sports Basketball,* Jerry Lucas cover, $11

Paperback book, *Basketball Stars of 1973,* Jerry West cover, $6

Program, 1947, College All-Stars vs. Indianapolis Kautskys, $75

Program, 1954, Harlem Globetrotters, $50

Program, 1977, NCAA Final Four Tournament, Atlanta, $12

Tickets, full book, 1990, Portland Trailblazers, playoffs, NBA finals, $195

Louis-Schmeling fight poster for taverns, ca. 1938. Photo courtesy of Hake's Americana & Collectibles.

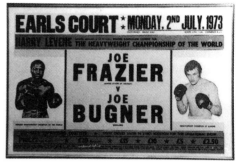

Site poster for Joe Frazier and Joe Bugner bout in 1973. Photo courtesy of Leland's Collectibles.

Boxing

Dressing-room pass, August 30, 1937, world heavyweight title fight, Joe Louis vs. Tommy Farr, New York City, mint condition, $125

Magazine, 1936, *Liberty,* Louis-Schmeling championship fight, $10

Poster, 1938, Louis-Schmeling fight for radio broadcasts, $150

Poster, 1973, Frazier-Bugner championship fight, $55

Football

Book, hardcover, 1968, *Playing Football to Win* by John Unitas, Doubleday & Co., $12

Cereal box, Wheaties, Dallas Cowboys, Super Bowl, 1993/94, $30

Full ticket, 1957, Gator Bowl, Tennessee vs. Texas A & M, mint condition, $30

Guide, 1904, *Spaulding's Official Football Guide* edited by Walter Camp, $90

Press pass, 1933, Notre Dame vs. Purdue, $65

Program, 1919 Rose Bowl, Pasadena, $1,500

Program, 1960, Navy vs. Villanova, homecoming, $20

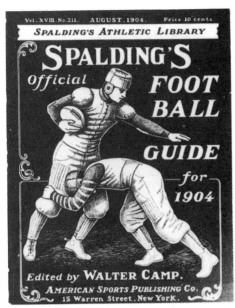

Spalding's Official Football Guide, *1904.*

Atlas football handbook, 1947, Standard service station.

Schedule, 1927, Maryville College, Tennessee, $35

Schedule booklet, 1947 official guide of American Football Coaches' Association, service station premium, $12

Ticket, 1928 game, Drake vs. Notre Dame, $165

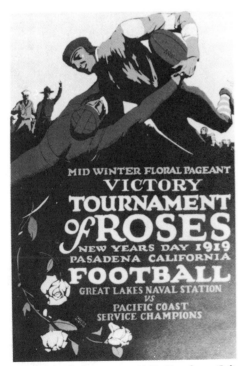

Rose Bowl football program, 1919, Pasadena, California.

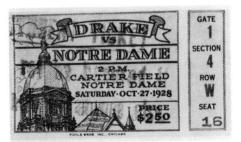

Notre Dame football ticket, 1928.

Hockey

Softcover book, *Hockey Stars of 1973,* New York Rangers cover, $5

Full set of tickets, Syracuse Eagles, 1974–75, American Hockey League, $10

Hardcover book, *Bobby Orr: My Game,* 1974, first edition, mint condition, $15

Magazine, *Legends Sports Memorabilia,* Wayne Gretzky cover, issue no. 15, $12

Ticket, Flyers, Stanley Cup playoffs, 1985, game three, $20

Horse Racing

Grandstand pass, 1962 Belmont Park, mint, $25

Press guide, 1956 Kentucky Derby, 144 pages, $100

Press pass, 1940 Hialeah Park race season, $5

Program, 1940 Kentucky Derby, Churchill Downs, 1939 winner on cover, $40

Season pass, 1950 Arlington Park clubhouse, $50

Tennis

Booklet, 1930s, *Tom Stow's Stroke Developer and System,* Wilson Sporting Goods, 16 pages, $8

Magazine, *Life,* September 20, 1968, Arthur Ashe cover, $25

Miscellaneous

Airplane racing poster, 1930 National Air Races, Chicago, $75

Golf, magazine, 1978, *Sports Illustrated,* Jack Nicklaus cover, $5

Olympics ticket, 1932 swimming, Los Angeles, $25

Parachute jumper postcard, 1935, Dorothy Darby, $20

National Air Races poster, 1930, Chicago, Illinois.

Real photo postcard of parachute jumper Dorothy Darby, 1935.

Greyhound racing program, 1946, Longwood, Florida.

Program, 1935, Col. W.T. Johnson's World's Championship Rodeo, Indianapolis, $18

Program, 1946, greyhound racing, Sanford-Orlando Kennel Club, Longwood, Florida, $6

Sports equipment catalog, 1936–37, *Spaulding for School and College Teams,* 100 pages, $50

Show program, 1961 International Livestock Expo & World's Championship Rodeo, Chicago, 144 pages, $20

Wrestling, full ticket, 1936, New York Coliseum, $25

TRADING CARDS

During the presidential election year of 1992, the wonderful people who produce Little Debbie Snack Cakes began printing presidential portrait cards on the bottom of some of the product boxes. It was a great idea. All that summer and into the fall, my wife and I sorted through boxes looking for all the presidents which made up the 39-card set. There were a few two-panel boxes and lots of three-panel boxes, and quite a variety of cakes to purchase in order to get all the presidents from George Washington to Ronald Reagan. We had to make the rounds week after week—from Wal-Mart to the grocery store—because not all of the various cakes were always stocked. At first we tried to just guess at which presidents we didn't have, later we became more sophisticated and wrote the names on paper, like grocery lists.

The time period of the Little Debbie series was perfect because we were working on a book about trading cards and wanted to include not only the obvious issues but the obscure ones as well. So every week we filled the grocery cart with boxes, and then spent the evening cutting them out as neatly as we could. In the beginning not many people had heard about the presidential sets, certainly no dealers or advanced collectors who were used to the typical announcements of leading trading card companies, which distributed cards in the conventional ways through supermarkets and card stores.

As we gathered the cards, we didn't realize they were being altered from time to time. It seems that some of the "fun facts" provided with each president were not all that much fun for everyone. For example, Herbert Hoover was remembered for the Great Depression, Lyndon Johnson for the Vietnam conflict, and Richard Nixon for Watergate. The company received many negative comments about those "facts," including one published by a columnist for the *Washington Post.* As a result, the company began pulling the original cards and replacing them with kinder versions. In the revised cards Johnson was remembered for the "one man, one vote" decision and Nixon was recalled as holding office when man walked on the moon.

Blissfully unaware of the changes, we began sending out Little Debbie cards to dealers, collectors, and others who had been so helpful in providing material for the book. Our stock of cards dwindled to just a handful. As we went to press with the book, none of the leading trading card magazines had mentioned them or priced them. We listed them in the book at 25 to 30¢ for a single card and $10 to $12 for the entire 39-card set, which was just about what it would take to purchase all the boxes—if you were lucky enough to find them all.

In the fall of 1993, more than a year after distribution, a brief article appeared on the Little Debbie cards in the trade publication *The Wrapper.* Written by Ron Wilson, considered the country's most distinguished researcher and historian on trading cards, it noted the cards had been changed after being distributed in pretty limited numbers in the first place. Wilson came up with what amounted to a 50-card set, including the original 39 and 11 revisions. (The Gerald Ford card was changed three different times.)

"A good collector's set has personality," wrote Wilson. "This personality can be created by several different means. One way is if the cards in the set can only be obtained a few at a time. Another is if the set offers something unique. Thirdly, a set acquires a character of it's own if it has variations to be collected, particularly if there is a good story behind the differences to be found. For all three of these reasons, the Presidential Portrait set has personality." By early 1994, *Tuff Stuff's Collect,* one of the country's top trading card publications, was listing the 50-card set, which included the variations, at $85. Individual cards cut from the boxes were $1.50 each.

A somewhat simpler story developed that same year when Sears, Roebuck and Company issued a series of cards based on Craftsman tools. To me it seemed strange— presidents on cards is one thing, but tools? My son telephoned me to say he had picked up a few packages, but it was because he was a fan of the tools rather than the cards themselves. Like the Little Debbie cards, they did not attract much attention at the time, but suddenly they disappeared from the retail

outlets. With good information on them and excellent photography, they had apparently attracted more tool fans like my son than anyone would have ever suspected. Today the same cards go for $1 to $2 each, when they can be found; and the sets of 110 list at nearly $100. In 1993 Sears issued another set which also disappeared from the shelves fairly quickly and it, too, is now listed in the price guides, but nowhere near the original sleeper price of 1992.

Trading cards have been around for more than a century, but only in recent years have they found true status as paper collectibles. Many credit the glory days of the Desert Storm War as the single event which brought masses of people to trading cards, but, for whatever reason, people are now looking much more fondly at childhood heroes like Superman, Davy Crockett, Batman, and E.T., who all appeared on cards over the years. Cards from A-Team to Zorro are, in part, a culmination of 19th-century contributions, including fine photography and fancy printing. During the second half of that century, leading photographers like Matthew Brady began producing illustrations of famous people. Pasted on cardboard with a brief advertisement on the back, they became known as cartes de visite or cards of visit. In a very short time, they were warmly welcomed as collectibles. Following the Civil War, chromolithograph printing had developed enough to make available to the public elaborately colored trade cards. Louis Prang (mentioned earlier for his pioneer contributions to greeting cards) published a series of card-sized portraits of popular war generals which sold for 10¢ each. They sold in the millions and prompted another Prang set on American birds. Soon Prang was joined by competitors who also sought to profit from the nation's buding romance with splendid color.

By the 1880s there was still another type of card to choose from—the cigarette card. Once used to simply protect the cigarettes from being bent and crushed, pictures on these cards ranged from bike riders to burlesque performers and from heroic dogs to women in professional occupations. Even before the turn of the century, a card collector could select from battle scenes, clipper ships, comic characters, presidential candidates, flowers, and both Roman and Greek goddesses. The widely varied selections— allowing for the fact that movies and TV did not yet exist—were not all that different from today's trading card choices.

During the early 20th century even baking soda companies got into the business of offering trading cards as premiums. Products provided sparkling topical cards as a bonus to those who purchased the packages. In the Depression years of the 1930s, there was a surprising new surge of trading cards, which, this time, was led by candy and gum manufacturers. The decade just before the outbreak of World War II saw the introduction of many cards which are considered classic today. One of the most prolific companies was Indian Gum, which issued sets, each incorporating more than 200 cards. A few other great issues of that time included Foreign Legion, Boy Scouts, and Walt Disney. Mickey Mouse bubble gum cards were issued by a firm in Philadelphia in a 96-card series in the 1930s. Eventually, two albums with different covers were provided to house each group of 48 cards. The albums each sold for 5 gum wrappers and 5¢. Immediately after the first series, the company followed with Mickey Mouse With the Movie Stars, a set of 24 showing Mickey greeting film greats in caricature form. A few years later the Overland Candy Company offered a large-sized series of Walt Disney pictures. The set included an illustration of Mickey Mouse from the cartoon *Brave Little Tailor,* a 1938 release. Nearly 50 years later, Impel included a scene from the same feature as part of their Disney set.

War fever was at its peak in the late 1930s and early 1940s, and like the 1990s when at least 15 different firms produced Desert Storm cards, there were a number of war card sets. Among the most memorable were Fighting Planes, Horrors of War, War Gum, Warships, America at War, Uncle Sam,

and Zoom Airplanes. A few fictional heroes did slip in during those dark days, as when a candy company issued a set of Dick Tracy cards in a 1¢ package of caramel candy and Superman appeared both on the backs on candy boxes and on gum cards.

In the relatively peaceful climate of the late 1940s, sets such as America Salutes the FBI and those featuring movie stars prevailed among card selections. In 1947 the Bond Bread Company of New York attempted to boost sales, as did many other companies around the country, by inserting movie star cards in each package. The black-and-white images of Betty Davis, Joan Crawford, George Raft, Cary Grant, Danny Kaye, and Jimmy Stewart were a big success, although the bread business eventually faltered.

Elvis Presley appeared on his first card set in 1956, but *Gunsmoke*'s James Arness made a far bigger impact as the number one card of TV Westerns. Early television spawned a major chapter in the life of trading cards of the 1950s as legends like Hopalong Cassidy moved from the big screen to the TV set and also into packages of Topps gum. Hoppy's cards are highly regarded today, as are most of the other 1950s cards, including the Three Stooges, Davy Crockett, Frontier Days, The Lone Ranger, World on Wheels, and space-related issues like jets, rockets, and spacemen.

The 1960s proved to be the golden age for many things, including monster cards. One of the finest monster sets was produced in 1961 by Nu-Cards. The 146-card set was called "Movie Monsters" on the wrappers, "Shock Monsters" on the boxes, and "Horror Monsters" by collectors. Nu-Card used actual photographs from hit monster movies and gave eager buyers the likes of Frankenstein, Creature from the Black Lagoon, Monster from Outer Space, and even the Bowery Boys Meet the Monsters. In the latter 1960s, Topps produced "Monster Laffs," which relied heavily on artwork from the early Monster Midgee cards of 1963, actual movie photos with humorous captions.

One of the most fabled trading cards sets

of the 20th century appeared as one of many popular monster-theme card sets in the 1960s. The horrific "Mars Attacks" cards came from original art provided by Norm Saunders. Currently the full set of 55 cards is worth hundreds of dollars and has even been sold in some of New York City's leading auction galleries. Saunders went on to provide the original art for the Batman card series of 1966. That year there were five different card sets which starred Batman and Robin. Other major TV-movie-related cards of the 1960s included Planet of the Apes, Daktari, and the Monkees.

In 1964 the Beatles appeared in several sets of gum cards, including two from the movie *Hard Day's Night,* one in color and one in black and white. The sets ranged from 55 to 64 cards. In 1967 Leaf issued the first of many *Star Trek* cards. An immediate legal dispute took place, and the 72-card set was quickly withdrawn from the market. As a result, the cards are scarce and treasured today. Other 1960s material popular with collectors are the monster-humor cards and those from TV shows such as *Addams Family, Flintstones, Flying Nun, Gomer Pyle, Rat Patrol,* and *Lost in Space.*

For still another perspective, consider the *Gilligan's Island* trading cards of the 1960s. If you have seen any lately, you are lucky, as they are probably the scarcest cards of that decade, and they have soared in value. The TV show about seven people shipwrecked on an island was not all that popular in the 1960s. It ran for three seasons on CBS—from September 1964 to September 1967—with lukewarm ratings. What made it a legend where the reruns. It is currently the top syndicated television program in the world, being continuously aired since the 1964 premier. In January of 1965 Topps issued the gum card set based on the show, using black-and-white scenes from the early TV episodes. The set was relatively short-lived for Topps, disappearing after a few months on the shelves. Some of the cast members were given little coverage on the cards. Russell Johnson as the professor was

only on three cards, Tina Louise as the movie star Ginger Grant was only on two cards, and Dawn Wells as the farm girl Mary Ann Summers was only on one card. All of these factors, plus the growing nostalgic romance with paper things of the 1960s, has placed these trading cards very high on the collector scale. Cards depicting the *Brady Bunch* (1970s) and *Hogan's Heroes* (1960s), are well regarded, but not like those of *Gilligan's Island.* Today the difficult-to-find cards sell for $12 to $14 each in good condition, with the entire set of 55 approaching $900.

One of the epic sets of the 1970s was *Star Wars.* Starting in 1977 Topps issued five trading card and sticker sets aimed at capturing the science-fiction glory of the movie that was *Star Wars.* Each set included 66 cards and 11 stickers, and the massive combination of 330 cards and 55 stickers was as immediately popular with the public as were the films. *Star Wars* cards spun some interesting stories, including one about card 207 in the fourth series. Ultimately there were two versions of the card (a fairly rare occurrence in trading card production at the time). The first was the now infamous x-rated C-3PO, which was recalled. A mischievous "mistake" was corrected and a new card issued to complete the set.

Another story about the *Star Wars* cards concerns film producer George Lucas and his personal preference regarding cards. Because Lucas is a diabetic, he requested that Topps offer sugar-free bubble gum with some of the *Star War* card issues, and they complied. This special item was sold with four different outside wrapper designs. The sugar-free gum 56-card set lists at about $75 today, and the single wrappers run from $1 to $2 each.

Americans spent millions of dollars on Desert Storm cards and virtually turned the corner on trading-card buying and collecting. In the 1990s card companies and various special interest groups were producing about 250 different sets of cards annually, with a special view for fantasy, art, and comic-book-related cards. Most current cards are available at retail outlets such as drugstores and toy stores. Issues within the last three or four years can often be found at specialty comic book and trading-card shops. Older cards, issued from 10 to 100 years ago, are typically sold by specialized dealers who advertise in trade publications. Several magazines (see Recommended Reading), available on newsstands or by subscription, list hundreds of current values on cards printed over the past 100 years.

Condition is, of course, important in trading cards. Cards prior to the 1960s will almost always have some signs of wear, but the best of the 1970s and 1980s can usually be found in near-mint condition. Prior to the 1980s, young collectors typically used rubber bands to hold the full sets together. As a result, the condition of the first and last cards of many series is often not as good as that of other cards of the series.

Trading cards, which have yet to approach the tidal wave of popularity of baseball cards, can still be found in garage sales, flea markets, and in a few closets back home.

Batman *TV series, 1966, Topps trading card.*

RECOMMENDED READING

Collector's Guide to Trading Cards by Robert Reed, Collector Books.

News, Views & Price Trends, monthly magazine, 19 Lores Plaza-Box 160, New Milford, CT 06776.

Non-Sports Update, bimonthly magazine, PO Box 5858, Harrisburg, PA 17110-0858.

Card Collector's Price Guide, monthly magazine, 155 E. Ames Ct. Plainview, NY 11803.

Tuff Stuff's Collect, monthly magazine, PO Box 1637, Glen Allen, VA 23060.

The Wrapper, eight issues per year, 7 Simpson St., Apt. A, Geneva, IL 60134.

PRICE LISTINGS

Batman TV series, 1966, Topps, puzzle back, single: $4, set of 44: $180

Beatles, 1964, Topps, black-and-white series, single: $2, set of 60: $150

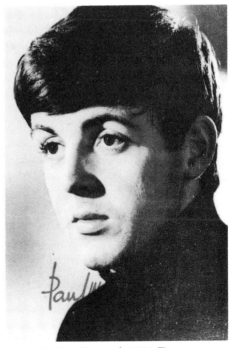

Beatles series I trading card, 1964, Topps.

Boy Scouts, 1933, Goudey, single: $15, set of 48: $850

Bring 'Em Back Alive, Topps, 1954, single: $4, set of 100: $400

Craftsman Tools, 1992, Sears, single: $1, set of 110: $118

Dallas, 1981, Donruss, single: 25¢, set of 56: $12

Davy Crockett, 1956, Topps, orange back, single: $3.50, set of 80: $300

Desert Storm Homecoming, 1991, Topps, single: 15¢, set of 88 with 11 stickers: $7

Fish series, 1900, Church & Dwight, single: $3.25, set of 30: $115

Gilligan's Island, 1965, Topps, single: $13, set of 55: $900

Happy Days, 1976, Topps, single: 15¢, set of 44 with 11 stickers: $14

Hit Stars of 1957, Topps, single: $6, set of 88: $700 (individual price of some big stars considerably higher)

Hogan's Heroes, 1966, Fleer, single: $8, set of 66: $620

Interesting Animals, 1892, Church & Dwight, single: $6, set of 60: $350

Jets, 1956, Topps, single: $3, set of 240: $400

Johnson vs. Goldwater, 1964, Topps, single: $2, set of 66: $65

Lost in Space, 1966, Topps, single: $5, set of 55: $325

Hit stars of 1957, Topps, George Shearing trading card.

Fish series, Church & Dwight Co., 1900 trading card.

Lost in Space, *1966, Topps trading card.*

Mars Attacks, 1962, Bubbles/Topps, single: $15, set of 55: $1,300

M.A.S.H., 1982, Donruss, single: 25¢, set of 66: $18

McHale's Navy, 1965, Fleer, single: $1.50, set of 66: $75

Mickey Mouse, 1937, Gum Inc., single: $20, set of 96: $2,000

Milk-Bone Superstars, 1993, Milk-Bone, single: 75¢, set of 20: $10

Mod Squad, 1969, Topps, single: $2.50, set of 55: $125

Monster Laffs, 1966, Topps, single $1, set of 66: $80

Mork and Mindy, 1978, Topps, single: 25¢, set of 99 with 22 stickers: $25

Movie Stars, 1947, Bond Bread, Single: $6, set of 34: $180

National Flags, 1910, Helmar, single: $2.50, set of 154: $385

Planet of the Apes, 1968 (movie), Topps, single: $2, set of 44: $85

Presidential Portraits, 1992, Little Debbie, single: $1.50, set of 39: $65, variation set of 50: $85 (two different fronts on 9 cards, three different on one card)

Rat Patrol, 1966, Topps, single: $1.50, set of 66: $75

Sergeant Preston of the Yukon, 1956, Quaker Oats, single: $5, set of 36: $155

Star Trek, 1967, Leaf, single: $25, set of 72: $1,500

Tarzan, Philadelphia Gum, 1966, single: $3, set of 66: $170

Time Marches On, 1940, maker unknown, single: $5, set of 48: $280

Treasure Island, 1960, Buymore, single: $1, set of 60: $60

TV Western Stars, 1960, Nu-Card, single: $3.50, set of 64: $135

Danny Kaye, Bond Bread, movie star cards, 1947.

Planet of the Apes, *1968, Topps movie trading card.*

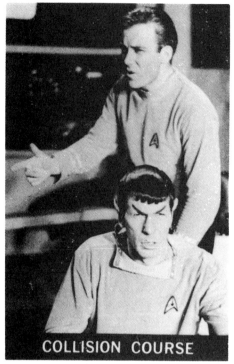

COLLISION COURSE

Star Trek, *1967, Leaf trading card.*

Tarzan, *1966, Philadelphia Gum trading card.*

U.S. Presidents, 1976, Ed-U-Cards, single: $1.50, set of 36: $45

War Gum, 1941, Gum Inc., single: $10, set of 132: $1,600

Wings, 1953, Topps, single: $2.50, set of 200: $550

World on Wheels, 1953, Topps, single: $3, set of 160: $450

X-Men, 1991, Comic Images, single: 25¢, set of 90: $20

Yule Laff, 1960, Fleer, single: $2, set of 66: $150

Zorro, 1958, Topps, single: $4.50, set of 88: $325

INDEX